THE BUDGET-FRIENDLY
VEGAN COOKBOOK

THE BUDGET-FRIENDLY
VEGAN
COOKBOOK

Healthy Meals for a Plant-Based Diet

ALLY LAZARE

Photography by Tom Story

ROCKRIDGE
PRESS

For Aaron, Audrey, and Autumn—my "A Team."
Thank you for inspiring me and sharing this journey
with me. I love you to the moon and back.

For general information on our other products and services or to obtain technical support, please contact our Customer Care Department within the U.S. at (866) 744-2665, or outside the U.S. at (510) 253-0500.

Rockridge Press publishes its books in a variety of electronic and print formats. Some content that appears in print may not be available in electronic books, and vice versa.

Interior and Cover Designer: Jill Lee
Photo Art Director/Art Manager: Karen Williams
Editor: Morgan Shanahan and Claire Yee
Production Editor: Ashley Polikoff
Photography © 2020 Tom Story. Food styling by Karen Shinto.
ISBN: Print 978-1-64611-917-2 | eBook 978-1-64611-918-9
R0

CONTENTS

Kitchen Sink Buckwheat Ramen, 148

INTRODUCTION

HELLO! Thank you so much for joining me on this budget-friendly vegan culinary journey. I'm excited to share a bunch of my favorite vegan dishes with you and get you excited about cooking them.

There are so many great plant-based options available to us all right now, from make-at-home recipes to restaurant dishes and from packaged foods to fast food and more. However, it can still be difficult to navigate the sea of vegan choices, for both new vegans and experienced ones. After all, it's hard to resist the temptation to buy a plant-based version of your favorite junk food, and it's easy to fall into eating vegan foods with little nutritional value, like a quick bowl of pasta. In the long run, though, that's not healthy for your body or your wallet.

If you've recently converted to a plant-based diet, it can be overwhelming figuring out what to eat on a daily basis, let alone how to shop for ingredients and how to prepare dishes. If you were previously an omnivore, you probably didn't think much about where you got protein in your diet. Now, protein sources might feel like the number one concern on your mind. Even if you've been vegan for years and are used to finding plant-based workarounds, it can be easy to get stuck in a rut of making the same few dishes over and over until you're in desperate need of change.

That's where this book comes in! I've created delicious, easy recipes that rely on readily available, healthy ingredients that won't strain your budget or keep you in the kitchen for hours on end.

When my family transitioned to a vegan diet almost 10 years ago, we had no idea where to start. We wanted dishes that were familiar to us but that didn't use animal products. It became my mission to re-create our old favorites, so I took everything I knew about cooking and turned it on its head. I looked at ingredients I already cooked with and figured out how to use them in new ways to re-create old flavors I loved and come up with new ones. And now, I'm sharing those creations with you.

It doesn't matter what your experience level is in the kitchen or how long you've been eating vegan. The recipes in this book all follow three simple rules: Each dish must 1) be easy to make, 2) use as many everyday ingredients as possible, and 3) taste delicious!

I hope my recipes and the stories behind them encourage you to get creative in the kitchen and to one day share your own culinary creations. **ENJOY!**

1

The Budget-Friendly Vegan

I'm often asked if following a vegan lifestyle is expensive. There are ways to eat expensively and frugally, no matter what type of lifestyle you follow—and the vegan lifestyle is no exception. In this book, I'll share several tips and tricks for cooking healthy, delicious vegan meals that use a wide variety of affordable plant-based proteins to maximize your meal planning ability and minimize your budget and prep time.

Eating a Balanced Vegan Diet without Breaking Your Budget

It's an exciting time to be vegan. There are new plant-based meat, egg, milk, and cheese substitutes available in mainstream supermarkets every day. Fancy plant-based products can be enticing, but they're also expensive, don't stretch as far (for batch cooking or doubling recipes), and are often heavily processed. They can also be limiting if you're trying to avoid soy or nuts.

Maintaining a vegan diet on a budget doesn't have to be a struggle, though, and you don't need to subsist on carbohydrate-heavy fillers like pasta or rice. The recipes in this book are healthy and delicious and incorporate a wide variety of affordable plant-based proteins you can find at almost any regular grocery store.

Low Cost, High Protein

New vegans sometimes struggle to reintegrate protein into their diet without meat and cheese. Getting too little protein on a long-term basis can leave you tired, hungry, and reaching for carb-heavy substitutes, which give you quick energy highs and equally big crashes later. A carbohydrate-heavy and protein-deficient diet can lead to fatigue, weight fluctuations, and high cholesterol. It's easier than you think to add nutrient-dense, plant-based proteins into your diet. Here's a list of low cost, protein-rich staples I love to keep in my kitchen:

- Chickpeas
- Lentils
- Beans
- Almonds
- Tofu
- Quinoa

VEGAN ABUNDANCE: A NUTRIENT-RICH DIET

Maintaining a healthy, well-balanced diet can be challenging. It can be difficult to figure out what you should be eating regularly and what you should avoid. When my family and I first went vegan, we relied heavily on a) packaged, processed vegan foods and b) carbohydrate-heavy meals. We were new to veganism and thought that being vegan meant switching to processed meat and cheese substitutes. We also replaced meat dishes with high-carb, low-nutrient meal "fillers" like pasta. We spent a lot of money—our grocery bills nearly doubled—and we didn't feel physically healthy.

While relying on packaged foods and carb replacements may seem "easier," there are long-term consequences. Processed foods, in addition to being expensive, are higher in salt, fat, sugar, and calories—all of which can have adverse effects on your body. Carb-heavy meals like pasta are cheap and filling, but they won't give you the nutrients you need.

Instead, base your meals around affordable protein-rich staples, like canned chickpeas or beans, supplemented with spices and cheap and healthy vegetables like carrots, celery, tomatoes, and zucchini. For the same cost as a bowl of pasta, you can put a hearty bowl of chili on the table. Both your body and your wallet will thank you!

Economical Meal Planning, Economical Cooking

Over the years, I've spent more than I care to admit on groceries that I never used because it was easier to just order a pizza. Eventually, I got tired of throwing away money and came up with some time-saving and budget-friendly tricks to avoid reaching for takeout menus or frantically dashing out to the grocery store at five p.m. every day.

1. Look in cookbooks and online for easy, plant-based recipes that inspire you. Save them on your phone or print them out and keep them handy.

2. Create a weekly meal plan with those recipes (bonus points if those meals can be doubled for lunch leftovers)!

3. Choose meals with overlapping ingredients. If three of your dinners require a grain, consider using variations on the same grain (like quinoa cooked or seasoned three different ways).

4. Write a shopping list. Include weekly staples that you know you'll need and recipe ingredients for the week.

5. Avoid expensive, processed packaged meat alternatives. Opt for whole-food, protein-rich choices, like tofu or legumes/beans.

6. Cook large amounts of prep ingredients ahead of time (like the quinoa mentioned in tip 3) so they're ready to go once daily dinner prep rolls around.

What to Buy Where

Depending on where you live, you may have few or several options for grocery shopping. For everyday staples—and most of the recipes in this book—your local grocery store is your best bet.

Grocery stores have constant sales—especially if you live in a densely populated urban area where chains are competing for your business. Most stores publish a weekly newspaper insert with weekly deals, and many have phone apps that you can reference as well. Look at these when shopping for the items on your weekly shopping list. In addition, many stores will match their competitors' prices if you can show them evidence of the price difference.

During the growing season, farmers' markets are a great place to buy high-quality, produce at a low price. You can also meet your local farmers and ask them questions about the best ways to prepare and store produce to maintain freshness.

Grocery Store Shopping

The vast majority of the ingredients in this book can be purchased at the grocery store. Here are the staple items I purchase:

* Canned chickpeas, beans, and lentils: While it might seem economical to buy these dried and in bulk, dried beans require soaking overnight or cooking for up to a few hours before you can use them in a recipe. One exception—for soups and stews I use dried lentils (they are a great way to thicken a soup and take on the soup's flavor).

* Tofu and tempeh

* Fresh fruit and vegetables (unless in season at the farmers' market)

* Frozen fruit and vegetables

* Breads, buns, and wraps

* Dried herbs and spices: These are shelf-stable, but they still lose flavor over time, so buy in small quantities rather than in bulk. Buy larger sizes of the top three to five spices—like salt and pepper—that you use daily.

* Jarred sauces and condiments: I've shared some recipes in this book for homemade versions of basic condiments, but I sometimes use store-bought versions to save money and time.

* Plant-based milks: canned coconut milk and cartons of soy, almond, or other milk alternatives

Farmers' Market Shopping

When in season, farmers' markets are a great place to buy fresh-picked produce at very reasonable prices. These are some of my favorite market picks:

- Cucumbers
- Peppers
- Tomatoes
- Green and wax beans
- Zucchini and squash
- Eggplant
- Potatoes
- Onions
- Carrots
- Corn
- Apples

Bulk Shopping

I like keeping large quantities of these items on hand in my pantry. They have long shelf lives, are easy to store, and I use them pretty much every day. I may purchase them at a wholesale store or at a local bulk food store.

- Oats
- Quinoa
- Rice
- Barley
- Couscous
- Nutritional yeast
- Dried lentils and peas, for soup
- Bread crumbs or panko
- Peanut and almond butters
- Tahini

SOME THINGS ARE JUST WORTH THE MONEY

One of the most common questions I get asked about budget-friendly meal planning is: What's more economical, homemade or store-bought? I'm a firm believer in working smarter, not harder, and making the best use of my time in the kitchen. While I am a huge supporter of using homemade items whenever possible, I'm also practical, and there are some staples in my pantry that are just easier (and less expensive in the long run) to buy instead.

Vegan cheese is one of those items. While making your own vegan cheese at home can be a fun experiment, it takes a long time and can require several expensive ingredients, like nuts and thickening agents. Nowadays, vegan cheese is easy to find at most mainstream grocery stores, and it has a longer shelf life than homemade vegan cheese. For cheeses that slice or shred, I recommend the brand Daiya, which is available in most stores, comes in a wide variety of flavors, and is soy-, gluten-, and nut-free.

For the same reasons, I also recommend purchasing (rather than making) other store-bought dairy replacements, such as plant-based milks, yogurts, butter, and sour cream. There are tons of budget-friendly versions of all these vegan staples available at most grocery stores as well.

Supply List

Now that we've covered the basics of how to meal plan, what to buy, and where to buy it, let's talk about the tools we need to make delicious, budget-friendly plant-based meals. You don't need to have a state-of-the-art kitchen to prepare any of the recipes in this book. They are designed to work with even the most basic of kitchen tools.

Necessary Kitchen Tools

APPLIANCES

- Oven
- Stovetop
- Refrigerator
- Freezer

TOOLS

- Knives (one large chef's knife and one or two smaller knives)
- Large cutting board
- Can opener
- Spatula
- Mixing spoon
- Whisk
- Measuring cups and spoons
- Mixing bowls (2 or 3)
- Box grater
- Colander or strainer

COOKWARE

- A deep/wide sauté pan or skillet (nonstick, stainless steel, or cast iron)
- A deep pot with a lid, for soups
- Large rimmed baking sheets
- Oven-safe baking dish (9 by 9 inches or 9 by 11 inches)
- Muffin tin

FOR STORAGE: airtight food storage containers

Nice-to-Have Kitchen Tools

- Microwave
- Electric kettle
- Blender or immersion blender
- Food processor
- Crock-pot or slow cooker
- Parchment paper or silicone baking sheets, to protect metal baking sheets (if you don't have these, use cooking spray, vegan butter, or oil)
- Extra pots or pans with lids
- Measuring glass (for liquid measuring)
- Electric hand mixer or stand mixer
- Wire cooling racks

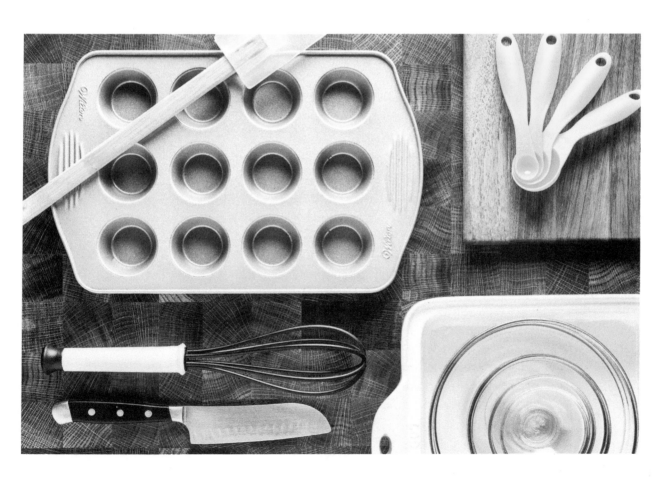

THE BATTLE OF BULK

Buying in bulk makes sense if you have a large family or if there are certain items you use every day. But at some point, bulk isn't worth it. Club-size products may seem like a deal, but before you buy, think your groceries through. The first questions I ask myself before I buy anything in bulk are:

- Do we really need that much of a particular item?
- Are we likely to eat it **all** before it expires, or will part of it end up going to waste? (This is particularly important for perishable items.)
- Where can I store bulk quantities of this item? Do I have space for it? Will I remember to use it?

If the answer to any of these questions is no, then skip it. Chances are, it'll be on sale again the next time you need it.

Stocking Your Pantry

Creating and sticking to a meal plan is always easier when you have all the components on hand and ready to use. There's nothing worse than getting halfway through a recipe and realizing you've run out of a basic staple. Here's a list of items I always keep in my kitchen:

- Cooking oils: grapeseed oil, vegetable or canola oil, extra-virgin olive oil, and coconut oil
- Basic seasonings: salt, pepper, onion powder, garlic powder, chili powder, paprika, oregano, basil, curry powder, and cinnamon
- Nutritional yeast
- Extra-firm tofu and tempeh
- Vegan milk alternatives: canned coconut milk, unsweetened (not vanilla) soy milk, and almond milk

- Vegan cheese alternatives: one block, one bag of shreds, and one container of dairy-free cream cheese
- Vegan butter
- Vegetable broth and vegetable bouillon cubes
- Grains: rice, quinoa, pasta, couscous, rolled oats
- Breads: tortillas, bread
- Canned beans and legumes: kidney beans, black beans, refried beans, chickpeas, lentils
- Canned diced tomatoes, tomato purée, and tomato paste
- Nut and seed butters: peanut butter (smooth and crunchy), almond butter, tahini
- Fresh vegetables: onions, garlic, potatoes, carrots, lettuce, celery
- Fresh fruits: lemons, limes, bananas
- Jarred pasta sauce
- Bread crumbs
- Soy sauce and hot sauce

FOR BAKING

- All-purpose flour
- Sugar: granulated sugar, powdered sugar, brown sugar
- Flaxseed (to make an egg replacement)
- Baking soda, baking powder
- Vegan butter
- Nut butters and nuts
- Fruits: bananas, dates

How to Use This Book

When my family and I started eating vegan, we had to relearn how to integrate sufficient protein into our diet. Instead of breaking the book down by meal types (soups, salads, main dishes, etc.), the recipes are sorted by protein source. Each chapter focuses on how you can use a given protein in a variety of well-balanced, nutritious vegan breakfasts, lunches, dinners, and snacks. My hope is that you'll be able to use this book to keep your weekly meal plans fresh and exciting, no matter what protein you have on hand.

THE FRUGAL COMMUNITY

Staying on-budget when meal planning doesn't just mean buying food on sale or choosing no-name instead of leading brands. It can also mean coming up with other ways to be economical.

Dinner groups. Gather a small group of vegan friends and plan out a meal. Have everybody bring one dish big enough to share, and suddenly you've got a well-rounded meal but had to shop for and prepare only one recipe.

Shop together. Grab a fellow vegan and hit the grocery store together. Look for items that you're both purchasing, and see if anything can be shared. Need only three carrots for a recipe, but the bags come with six? Buy one bag and split it.

Join a food co-op or community garden. Food co-ops are small grocery stores that are collectively owned by the members who shop there. Members are able to connect directly with local farmers and have a say in which products are stocked (and their price points). You can buy a membership or work in the store in exchange for membership. Community gardens rent affordable small plots of land so you can learn to grow your own food and even trade with others in the garden.

About the Recipes

Within these pages, you'll find ideas, inspiration, and recipes for meals that are:

Budget-friendly. You'll use similar ingredient groups for several meals to cut down on ingredient waste and learn tips on how to shop economically.

Time-sensitive. The majority of the recipes in this book can be made in 30 to 45 minutes or less.

Organized by protein source. The recipes are grouped by the main protein or vegan staple featured so you can easily identify recipes based on an ingredient you want to use or have on hand.

Clearly labeled. Each recipe contains at-a-glance dietary information, prep and cook times, necessary ingredients, and tips to stretch, enhance, use different techniques, or adapt the recipe to meet specific dietary restrictions or allergies (like nuts and gluten).

Focused on healthy, natural proteins. The recipes provided rely on natural protein sources that are high in nutrients and low in cost. There are no recipes with expensive, processed meat alternatives in this book.

And please remember, for all recipes in this book that are gluten-free, always check ingredient packaging for gluten-free labeling before purchasing in order to ensure foods, especially oats, were processed in a completely gluten-free facility.

2

Staples, Sauces, and Dressings

Tofu Chorizo Crumble

MAKES
2 CUPS

PREP TIME
5 MINUTES

COOK TIME
30 MINUTES

PER SERVING

CALORIES:
460

TOTAL FAT:
34 G

CARBS:
14 G

FIBER:
8 G

PROTEIN:
37 G

CALCIUM:
1029 MG

VITAMIN D:
0 MCG

VITAMIN B12:
0 MCG

IRON:
11 MG

ZINC:
4 MG

Crumbled tofu is a versatile substitute for ground meat. This chili-spiced tofu "chorizo" crumble is my go-to ground meat alternative for most Tex-Mex recipes. It's easy to make and lasts for 3 to 4 days in the refrigerator. The tofu is seasoned with a blend of several seasonings that I call "Tex-Mex Spice Mix." I like to make a large batch of the spice mixture ahead of time and keep it in the pantry for convenient use.

1 tablespoon canola or
  vegetable oil
1 teaspoon soy sauce
1 tablespoon chili powder
1 teaspoon cumin
1 teaspoon garlic powder
1 teaspoon paprika

½ teaspoon dried oregano
½ teaspoon onion powder
¼ teaspoon salt
¼ teaspoon pepper
1 (12-ounce) block extra-firm tofu,
  drained and pressed

1. Preheat your oven to 350°F. Line a large rimmed baking sheet with parchment paper.

2. In a small bowl, combine the oil, soy sauce, chili powder, cumin, garlic powder, paprika, dried oregano, onion powder, salt, and pepper and stir until the mixture becomes a paste. Set aside.

3. In a large bowl, crumble the tofu into small pieces. Add the spice paste to the tofu and toss until the tofu is thoroughly coated.

4. Spread onto the lined baking sheet in a single layer and bake for 30 minutes, removing the tray to stir the tofu every 10 minutes.

5. Cool completely and store in an airtight container. Refrigerate for up to 5 days or freeze for up to 3 months.

SUBSTITUTION TIP: To make this recipe gluten-free, swap the soy sauce for tamari.

Meaty Tofu Crumble

MAKES
2 CUPS

PREP TIME
5 MINUTES

COOK TIME
30 MINUTES

I use this crumble for Bolognese sauce, lasagna, or any dish that needs a ground meat substitute. This is my base recipe, but you can customize it to adapt to different recipes by swapping out the seasonings. For example, remove the paprika and add thyme and fennel. You can also add cumin and ground coriander and use it on a hummus platter or as an alternate filling in the Soy Curl Shawarma Wrap (page 60).

1 tablespoon canola or
    vegetable oil
1 teaspoon soy sauce
1 tablespoon dried oregano
1 tablespoon dried basil
¼ teaspoon red pepper flakes
    (or more if you want it spicy!)

½ teaspoon smoked paprika
½ teaspoon garlic powder
½ teaspoon onion powder
¼ teaspoon salt
¼ teaspoon ground black pepper
1 (12-ounce) block extra-firm tofu,
    drained and pressed

PER SERVING

CALORIES:
512

TOTAL FAT:
32 G

CARBS:
19 G

FIBER:
7 G

PROTEIN:
38 G

CALCIUM:
629 MG

VITAMIN D:
0 MCG

VITAMIN B12:
0 MCG

IRON:
9 MG

ZINC:
0 MG

1. Preheat your oven to 350°F. Line a large rimmed baking sheet with parchment paper.

2. In a small bowl, combine the oil, soy sauce, oregano, basil, red pepper flakes, paprika, garlic powder, onion powder, salt, and pepper. Mix until they form a paste. Set aside.

3. In a large bowl, crumble the tofu into small chunks. Toss with the spice paste until all the tofu pieces are coated. Spread the tofu onto the rimmed baking sheet in a single, even layer.

4. Bake for 30 minutes, stopping to toss the crumble every 10 minutes.

5. Cool completely and store in an airtight container in the fridge for up to 4 days.

STRETCH TIP: This tofu crumble freezes well, so if you're not using the entire batch, store it in a freezer-safe bag for up to 3 months.

Smoky Tofu "Bacon"

MAKES
12 SLICES

PREP TIME
5 MINUTES

COOK TIME
15 MINUTES

PER SERVING

CALORIES:
513

TOTAL FAT:
30 G

CARBS:
27 G

FIBER:
4 G

PROTEIN:
40 G

CALCIUM:
268 MG

VITAMIN D:
0 MCG

VITAMIN B12:
0 MCG

IRON:
7 MG

ZINC:
1 MG

This savory treat uses liquid smoke—which you can find at most grocery stores and online—to achieve a smoky flavor in a short amount of time. I created it to accompany a tofu scramble, but it can be used almost anywhere. It makes an amazing addition to the Avocado Superfood Salad (page 107), Potato Corn Chowder (page 102), or chili—that is, if you can stop yourself from eating it straight out of the pan!

2 tablespoons tamari

1 tablespoon maple syrup

1 teaspoon apple cider vinegar

3 drops liquid smoke

1 tablespoon extra-virgin olive oil

1 (12-ounce) block extra-firm tofu, drained and sliced into ½-inch strips

1. Make the marinade. In a small bowl, combine the tamari, maple syrup, vinegar, and liquid smoke.

2. Heat the oil in a large deep-frying pan over medium-high. When the oil is hot, add the tofu slices and sauté until golden brown on each side.

3. Add the marinade to the pan and continue to cook for 2 to 3 minutes or until almost all the liquid is gone and the tofu strips are sticky and caramelized.

4. Serve immediately or refrigerate in an airtight container for up to 4 days.

VARIATION TIP: Switch this up by using tempeh strips instead of tofu (follow the same cooking instructions). They add a deeper flavor and chewy texture that are delicious in a vegan BLT.

Quick Caramelized Onions

MAKES
1 CUP

PREP TIME
5 MINUTES

COOK TIME
15 MINUTES

Is there anything better than the smell of onions slowly caramelizing on the stove? I love using the deep, rich, and almost candy-like taste of caramelized onions to bring out the flavors in many dishes. What I don't love is standing over a stove for an hour waiting for them to cook. I came up with a cheat for those times you need that slow, simmered flavor in a hurry.

1 tablespoon vegan butter
2 tablespoons extra-virgin olive oil
5 cups thinly sliced onions
Water, as needed

1. In a heavy-bottomed stainless steel pan, melt the butter and oil together over high heat. Add the onions and cook, stirring constantly, for about 5 minutes or until sticky, caramelized brown spots coat the bottom of the pan.

2. Add 2 to 3 tablespoon of water. Using a wooden spoon, scrape up all the sticky bits. Repeat this process for about 15 minutes or until the onions are soft and have a deep, dark brown color. Remove from the heat immediately. Refrigerate in an airtight container for up to 3 days.

TECHNIQUE TIP: This recipe calls for both butter and oil—butter for its flavor and oil for its higher burn temperature. If you want to cut down on fats and oils, you can use butter only. If you do this, though, keep an extra-close eye on your onions as they cook, and add water frequently to prevent the onions from burning.

PER SERVING

CALORIES:
727

TOTAL FAT:
39 G

CARBS:
91 G

FIBER:
14 G

PROTEIN:
11 G

CALCIUM:
224 MG

VITAMIN D:
0 MCG

VITAMIN B12:
0 MCG

IRON:
2 MG

ZINC:
2 MG

Basic Curry Paste

MAKES
1 CUP

PREP TIME
10 MINUTES

COOK TIME
10 MINUTES

PER CUP

CALORIES:
401

TOTAL FAT:
29 G

CARBS:
35 G

FIBER:
11 G

PROTEIN:
6 G

CALCIUM:
136 MG

VITAMIN D:
0 MCG

VITAMIN B12:
0 MCG

IRON:
5 MG

ZINC:
1 MG

There are hundreds of varieties of curry—all different based on the types of herbs, spices, and heat used. Many curries start with curry paste. I love experimenting with different store-bought curry pastes, but it's also quite fun (and economical) to make your own. Try adding cumin powder to give your curry paste a smoky flavor, or use a vindaloo curry powder (instead of Madras) for a wicked-hot curry paste.

2 tablespoons extra-virgin olive oil
1 large onion, diced
3 garlic cloves, sliced
1 red chili, diced

2-inch piece ginger, peeled
  and sliced
2 tablespoons mild or Madras
  curry powder
2 tablespoons tomato paste

1. In a small, deep pan, heat the oil on medium-high. Add the onion, garlic, red chili, and ginger. Sauté for 5 to 6 minutes, or until soft and slightly browned.

2. Add the curry powder and tomato paste and simmer for 3 to 4 minutes.

3. Transfer to a blender or food processor and process until smooth.

4. Cool completely and refrigerate in an airtight container for up to two weeks.

STRETCH TIP: To stretch this recipe, double it and portion out the paste into an ice cube tray. Freeze it and pop a cube or two into dishes whenever you need it.

Easy 4-Ingredient Vegan Mayonnaise

Mayonnaise is a staple for countless dishes and is hard to live without! Thankfully, eggless mayo is incredibly easy to make. Prepackaged vegan mayonnaise is now widely available and relatively affordable, but many varieties are full of additives and preservatives. For this reason, I love to make my own four-ingredient mayo. It's inexpensive and easy to prepare and is a great addition to all kinds of delicious dishes.

MAKES
2 CUPS

PREP TIME
5 MINUTES

½ cup unsweetened soy milk, at room temperature

2 teaspoons apple cider vinegar or fresh lemon juice (juice of ½ lemon)

1 teaspoon salt, more to taste

1 cup oil, such as canola or vegetable

PER CUP

CALORIES:
1976

TOTAL FAT:
220 G

CARBS:
4 G

FIBER:
2 G

PROTEIN:
5 G

CALCIUM:
31 MG

VITAMIN D:
0 MCG

VITAMIN B12:
0 MCG

IRON:
1 MG

ZINC:
0 MG

1. Combine milk, vinegar, and salt in a blender or food processor, and blend on low for 5 to 10 seconds. With the blender still running, gradually pour in the oil, increasing in speed once all the oil is added. Continue blending until the mayonnaise has a thick consistency.

2. Add salt to taste. Adjust the consistency by adding more milk to thin it out or more oil to thicken, blending after each addition.

3. Refrigerate for up to 4 days in an airtight container.

VARIATION TIP: Feel free to play with added ingredients, like hot sauce or seasonings, to adjust the flavor in this mayo. Add a minced garlic clove or two to make garlic mayo. Or stir in spoonfuls of horseradish and Dijon mustard in at the end and top with Quick Caramelized Onions (page 19) on your favorite veggie burger!

MAKES
2 CUPS

PREP TIME
10 MINUTES

COOK TIME
40 MINUTES

PER SERVING

CALORIES:
901

TOTAL FAT:
77 G

CARBS:
58 G

FIBER:
31 G

PROTEIN:
12 G

CALCIUM:
145 MG

VITAMIN D:
0 MCG

VITAMIN B12:
0 MCG

IRON:
3 MG

ZINC:
3 MG

GLUTEN-FREE, NUT-FREE

Roasted Garlic Guacamole

This is my go-to guacamole for entertaining. It takes a little more time than regular guac, but it's worth the effort. The addition of roasted garlic pairs so well with the fattiness of the avocado and the tartness of lime and helps mellow out the heat from the jalapeño! I use this on nachos or as a dip on a vegan charcuterie board and mix it with my Easy 4-Ingredient Vegan Mayonnaise (page 21) to make an incredible sandwich spread.

2 heads garlic
1 tablespoon extra-virgin olive oil
3 large ripe avocados, pitted and
  cut into large chunks
½ cup red onion, diced
½ teaspoon onion powder

1 jalapeño, seeded and diced
2 tablespoons finely chopped fresh
  cilantro or flat-leaf parsley
1 tablespoon lime juice
Hot sauce, to taste
Salt and pepper, to taste

1. Preheat the oven to 400°F.

2. Slice the tops off the garlic heads so that the cloves inside are exposed but still attached to the bulb. Place each head of garlic on a sheet of aluminum foil and drizzle with the olive oil. Wrap the sides of the foil around the garlic to create pouches and twist the tops to seal them.

3. Bake for 30 to 40 minutes until the garlic is soft and brown. Allow to cool for 10 minutes before scooping the softened cloves into a small bowl. Set aside.

4. In a large bowl, mash the avocados until almost smooth, leaving a few chunks for texture. Add the roasted garlic, red onion, onion powder, jalapeño, cilantro, lime juice, hot sauce, salt, and pepper. Stir to combine. Cover and chill for 30 minutes before serving. If refrigerating, store in an airtight container covered with plastic wrap to prevent browning.

PREP TIP: Save time for future batches by roasting several garlic heads at once and freezing the remaining cloves in ice cube trays for use at a later date.

Pico de Gallo

MAKES
1½ CUPS

PREP TIME
15 MINUTES

Pico de gallo (also sometimes called salsa fresca) is a fresh, chopped salsa that is bursting with bright flavors. It's also a great base for other salsas, like peach or mango, and is a definite crowd-pleaser on nacho night. I recommend using fresh ingredients for this dish, including fresh jalapeños. Pico de gallo can be refrigerated in an airtight container for up to a week.

3 or 4 large plum tomatoes, seeded and diced
½ cup diced red onion
1 scallion, finely chopped
2 garlic cloves, minced
1 jalapeño, diced
½ cup cilantro or flat-leaf parsley, chopped
2 tablespoons lime juice
Salt and pepper, to taste

In a large bowl, combine the tomatoes, onion, scallion, garlic, jalapeño, cilantro, lime juice, salt, and pepper. Stir well to combine. Serve immediately or refrigerate in an airtight container for up to a week.

TECHNIQUE TIP: Jalapeños are the mildest of hot chili peppers, with great flavor and mildly intense heat. If you want their flavor but not all the heat, slice the pepper in half and scrape out the seeds and the white ribs inside before dicing. Remember to wash your hands and cutting board very well after using!

PER SERVING

CALORIES:
103

TOTAL FAT:
1 G

CARBS:
24 G

FIBER:
5 G

PROTEIN:
4 G

CALCIUM:
72 MG

VITAMIN D:
0 MCG

VITAMIN B12:
0 MCG

IRON:
1 MG

ZINC:
1 MG

Homemade BBQ Sauce

MAKES
3 CUPS

PREP TIME
5 MINUTES

COOK TIME
40 MINUTES

PER CUP

CALORIES:
1325

TOTAL FAT:
60 G

CARBS:
183 G

FIBER:
16 G

PROTEIN:
24 G

CALCIUM:
408 MG

VITAMIN D:
0 MCG

VITAMIN B12:
0 MCG

IRON:
15 MG

ZINC:
3 MG

A good homemade BBQ sauce is a game changer. And every cook has their personal "best ever" sauce. My dad has been making the same BBQ sauce for 30 years, and his recipe is a closely guarded secret. (I don't even know what's in it!) This recipe is smoky and sweet but doesn't have the high sugar content and preservatives of a store-bought version. This sauce keeps in the fridge for several weeks, so consider making a double batch!

¼ cup extra-virgin olive oil
½ large onion, diced
1 garlic clove, minced
½ cup tomato paste
½ cup apple cider vinegar
½ cup maple syrup
¼ cup mustard

½ cup soy sauce
2 tablespoons brown sugar
2 tablespoons chili powder
2 teaspoons ground cumin
¼ teaspoon ground cinnamon
¼ teaspoon ground cayenne
    pepper (optional)

1. Heat the oil in a large saucepan over medium-low heat. Add the onion and sauté for 5 to 7 minutes, or until soft and translucent but not browned. Add the garlic and cook for 30 seconds, stirring continuously to prevent burning.

2. Add the tomato paste, apple cider vinegar, maple syrup, mustard, soy sauce, brown sugar, chili powder, cumin, cinnamon, and cayenne, if using. Whisk to combine. Bring to a boil before reducing heat to low, and simmer, uncovered, for 30 minutes or until thick. Cool in glass jars and refrigerate.

SUBSTITUTION TIP: To make this BBQ sauce gluten-free, swap the soy sauce for tamari, which is a dark-brewed soy sauce made without wheat.

Vegan Cheddar Cheese Sauce

MAKES
2 CUPS

PREP TIME
5 MINUTES

COOK TIME
20 MINUTES

This is my classic mac-and-cheese sauce. This dish gets its start from a classic French béchamel sauce, which sounds fancy but is very easy to make. It also makes a great Alfredo sauce if you leave out the Cheddar shreds and ramp up the garlic! I use this sauce in other recipes in this book, like the Broccoli Cheddar Rice (page 150), Chorizo Stuffed Peppers with Rice (page 111), and Tempeh Breakfast Hash (page 44)

2 cups unsweetened soy milk

1 medium onion, roughly chopped

4 garlic cloves, peeled and smashed

1 tablespoon ground mustard

1 tablespoon nutritional yeast

½ teaspoon ground black pepper

2 tablespoons butter

2 tablespoons all-purpose flour

1 (8-ounce) package vegan Cheddar-style shreds

PER SERVING

CALORIES:
1174

TOTAL FAT:
81 G

CARBS:
85 G

FIBER:
7 G

PROTEIN:
25 G

CALCIUM:
828 MG

VITAMIN D:
240 MCG

VITAMIN B12:
8 MCG

IRON:
4 MG

ZINC:
2 MG

1. In a medium pot, heat the soy milk, onion, garlic, mustard, nutritional yeast, and pepper over medium heat, allowing the mixture to steam (but not boil). Once steaming, turn off heat and cover. Let the mixture steep for 15 minutes. Strain the mixture, reserving the seasoned soy milk and discarding the onion and garlic.

2. In a large pot, melt the 2 tablespoons of butter over medium-high heat. Using a wooden mixing spoon, add the 2 tablespoons of flour and stir constantly to fully incorporate and form a roux (flour and butter paste).

3. Once the roux forms, switch to a wire whisk. Slowly incorporate the steamed milk into the roux, stirring constantly, until the mixture thickens, 5 to 7 minutes.

4. Once the mixture is thick enough to coat the back of a spoon, remove from heat and whisk in the Cheddar-style shreds. Stir until completely mixed. Serve hot or allow to cool and refrigerate for up to 5 days in an airtight container.

SUBSTITUTION TIP: To make this sauce wheat-free, you can use gluten-free flour in the roux. If doing so, work quickly—gluten-free flour tends to absorb liquid faster than all-purpose flour, and you don't want your roux to dry up and burn.

Stovetop Enchilada Sauce

MAKES
3 CUPS

PREP TIME
10 MINUTES

COOK TIME
20 MINUTES

I love this enchilada sauce. It's bright, warm, and versatile, plus it smells amazing as it simmers on the stove. I keep a jar of it in the fridge and use it to add a smoky, spicy, tomato Tex-Mex punch to numerous dishes. You can adjust the heat by changing the amount of hot sauce in the recipe or by de-seeding and ribbing the jalapeño to remove spice.

PER SERVING

CALORIES:
638

TOTAL FAT:
32 G

CARBS:
85 G

FIBER:
23 G

PROTEIN:
14 G

CALCIUM:
346 MG

VITAMIN D:
0 MCG

VITAMIN B12:
0 MCG

IRON:
10 MG

ZINC:
2 MG

2 tablespoons vegetable oil
1 medium onion, diced
2 garlic cloves, minced
2 tablespoons chili powder
1 teaspoon onion powder
1 teaspoon ground cumin
¼ teaspoon smoked paprika

2 cups tomato sauce
1 (15-ounce) can diced tomatoes
1 jalapeño, diced
1 tablespoon maple syrup
½ teaspoon hot sauce (optional)
1 cup water

1. In a large saucepan, heat the oil over medium-high heat and sauté the onion until lightly golden. Add the garlic, chili powder, onion powder, cumin, and smoked paprika, and cook for 2 minutes, stirring occasionally.

2. Add the tomato sauce, diced tomatoes, jalapeño, maple syrup, hot sauce (if using), and water, and stir to combine. Bring to a boil. Adjust heat to low and simmer for 15 to 20 minutes.

3. Remove from heat. Purée the mixture in small batches in a blender or food processor until smooth. Alternatively, use an immersion blender in the saucepan to purée until smooth. Refrigerate for up to four weeks.

STRETCH TIP: This sauce keeps for up to four weeks. Consider making a double batch and storing it in the fridge or freezing in portion-controlled amounts in freezer-safe resealable bags. To defrost, submerge the bag in warm water until thawed.

White Garlic Dill Sauce

MAKES
1 CUP

PREP TIME
10 MINUTES

The first time I made this sauce, I tested it out on friends at a pizza and movie night. Some were vegan; some weren't. They were equally blown away by how rich and creamy this sauce was and how well it paired with the pizza. The next time I made it, I served it with my Buffalo-style Cauliflower Wings Two Ways (page 121), and again, it was perfect. Keep a jar of this in your fridge—you'll want to dip everything in it!

3 tablespoons vegan butter

3 to 4 garlic cloves, minced

¼ teaspoon salt

¼ teaspoon ground black pepper

¼ teaspoon dried oregano

3 tablespoons all-purpose flour

1 cup unsweetened soy milk

¼ cup nutritional yeast

2 tablespoons chopped fresh dill

1. In a small pan, melt the butter over medium heat. Once the butter is just melted, add the garlic and cook for 30 seconds. Add the salt, pepper, and oregano, and stir.

2. Whisk in the flour to create a roux (flour and butter paste). Slowly add the soy milk, whisking constantly, until the sauce thickens.

3. Remove the sauce from heat and stir in the nutritional yeast and dill. Chill for at least 30 minutes before serving. Refrigerate leftovers for up to 5 days in an airtight container.

VARIATION TIP: If you don't have any fresh dill or can't find it at your local supermarket, you can use 1 tablespoon dried dill instead. You can also adjust the amount of garlic to fit your taste preference.

PER SERVING

CALORIES:
582

TOTAL FAT:
38 G

CARBS:
35 G

FIBER:
10 G

PROTEIN:
26 G

CALCIUM:
143 MG

VITAMIN D:
0 MCG

VITAMIN B12:
10 MCG

IRON:
7 MG

ZINC:
5 MG

Stir-Fry Sauce

While store-bought sauces usually aren't expensive, they can be loaded with sugar and preservatives, so I like to make my own. This recipe for a multipurpose stir-fry sauce—which I often use as a vegan alternative to hoisin sauce—uses a specific kind of chili sauce called sambal oelek, which is available in the international section of most grocery stores. If you can't find it, you can use sriracha, sweet chili sauce, or any other hot sauce.

PER SERVING

CALORIES:
370

TOTAL FAT:
17 G

CARBS:
49 G

FIBER:
2 G

PROTEIN:
7 G

CALCIUM:
74 MG

VITAMIN D:
0 MCG

VITAMIN B12:
0 MCG

IRON:
2 MG

ZINC:
1 MG

1 tablespoon cornstarch
4 tablespoons cold water, divided
2 tablespoons soy sauce
2 teaspoons sesame oil
1 tablespoon apple cider vinegar
1 tablespoon lime juice
1 tablespoon smooth
  peanut butter

2 tablespoons maple syrup
1 teaspoon brown sugar
½ tablespoon minced ginger
2 garlic cloves, minced
½ teaspoon sambal oelek or other
  hot sauce

1. In a medium bowl, dissolve the cornstarch in 2 tablespoons of cold water. Add the soy sauce, remaining 2 tablespoons of water, sesame oil, vinegar, lime juice, peanut butter, maple syrup, brown sugar, ginger, garlic gloves, and sambal oelek. Whisk to combine.

2. Transfer the sauce to a small saucepan and bring it to a simmer over medium heat for about 5 minutes, stirring continuously, until sauce thickens. Remove from heat.

3. If storing, refrigerate in an airtight container for up to 1 week.

SUBSTITUTION TIP: You can make this sauce nut-free by swapping the peanut butter for soy butter, seed butter, or even tahini. You can also swap out the soy sauce for tamari to make this sauce gluten-free.

Teriyaki Sauce

MAKES
1½ CUPS

PREP TIME
10 MINUTES

Teriyaki sauce is a staple in Japanese (and Japanese-inspired) cooking and comes in handy for many of the dishes in this book. This version has lower amounts of sugar and salt, but you can adjust the levels of salt and sugar to your taste. This sauce also works as a marinade for tofu—submerge tofu in the sauce, cover, and refrigerate for at least an hour or overnight.

¼ cup soy sauce

1¼ cups cold water, divided

½ teaspoon grated fresh ginger

¼ teaspoon garlic powder

3 tablespoons brown sugar, packed

1 tablespoon maple syrup

2 tablespoons cornstarch

1. In a saucepan over medium heat, mix the soy sauce, 1 cup of water, ginger, garlic powder, brown sugar, and maple syrup.

2. In a small bowl, dissolve the cornstarch in the remaining ¼ cup of cold water and stir until no lumps are left. Add the cornstarch mixture to the saucepan. Stir until combined and simmer over medium heat until the sauce becomes thick and glossy. Remove from heat.

3. If storing, refrigerate in an airtight container for up to 1 week.

SUBSTITUTION TIP: Gluten-free teriyaki sauces can be hard to find or be very expensive at your local grocery store. Make this recipe gluten-free by swapping the soy sauce for tamari.

PER SERVING

CALORIES:
258

TOTAL FAT:
0 G

CARBS:
59 G

FIBER:
1 G

PROTEIN:
6 G

CALCIUM:
63 MG

VITAMIN D:
0 MCG

VITAMIN B12:
0 MCG

IRON:
2 MG

ZINC:
1 MG

Cream of Mushroom Sauce

MAKES
3 CUPS

PREP TIME
10 MINUTES

COOK TIME
10 MINUTES

PER SERVING

CALORIES:
522

TOTAL FAT:
32 G

CARBS:
41 G

FIBER:
9 G

PROTEIN:
23 G

CALCIUM:
69 MG

VITAMIN D:
7 MCG

VITAMIN B12:
10 MCG

IRON:
4 MG

ZINC:
6 MG

This recipe is somewhere between a sauce and a soup. It's thick, rich, and full of creamy mushroom flavor. It's a perfect replacement for old-fashioned cream of mushroom soup, but I've also served it on pasta and as a gravy on Garlic Chive Red Mashed Potatoes (page 162). The mushroom flavor deepens after cooking, so feel free to make it a day ahead and reheat it when needed.

2 tablespoons extra-virgin olive oil
1 medium onion, diced
8 ounces cremini mushrooms, thinly sliced (about 2½ cups)
1 cube vegetable bouillon
1 (14-ounce) can full-fat coconut milk
½ teaspoon ground mustard
¼ cup nutritional yeast
¼ teaspoon salt
¼ teaspoon black pepper
2 tablespoons all-purpose flour

1. Heat the oil in a large, deep pan over medium-high heat. Add the onion and sauté until translucent and beginning to brown. Add the mushrooms and continue to cook until they are golden brown. Add the bouillon cube and stir until dissolved.

2. Pour in the coconut milk, mustard, nutritional yeast, salt, and pepper. Stir to combine. Reduce to medium heat and simmer for 10 minutes.

3. Whisk in the flour and stir to dissolve. Simmer for 5 to 10 minutes or until the sauce is thick enough to coat the back of a spoon. Refrigerate for up to 3 days.

VARIATION TIP: I like to use cremini mushrooms because of their dark, earthy flavor, but this sauce also works well with milder white button mushrooms. If using white button mushrooms, cook them 5 to 10 minutes longer to allow their flavor to develop.

Spicy Peanut Sauce

MAKES
1 CUP

PREP TIME
10 MINUTES

This sauce is one of the easiest to make in this book. It makes a great base for pad Thai–style noodles, a marinade for a spicy tofu and veggie stir-fry, and a tasty dip for spring rolls and other appetizers. I recommend using chunky peanut butter to give the sauce some texture, especially when using as a dip. You can use any brand of sweet chili sauce available at your local supermarket.

½ cup sweet chili sauce
⅓ cup soy sauce
3 garlic cloves, minced

3 tablespoons chunky peanut butter
2 tablespoons lime juice
1 tablespoon granulated sugar

In a small bowl, combine the sweet chili sauce, soy sauce, garlic cloves, peanut butter, lime juice, and granulated sugar. Whisk to combine. If storing, refrigerate in an airtight container for up to 5 days.

STRETCH TIP: To temper the heat in this sauce a bit or stretch it into other uses, mix in a can of coconut milk. It gives the sauce a creamy texture that is delicious on rice noodles.

PER SERVING

CALORIES:
568

TOTAL FAT:
24 G

CARBS:
74 G

FIBER:
5 G

PROTEIN:
21 G

CALCIUM:
88 MG

VITAMIN D:
0 MCG

VITAMIN B12:
0 MCG

IRON:
3 MG

ZINC:
1 MG

MAKES
3 CUPS

PREP TIME
10 MINUTES

COOK TIME
25 MINUTES

PER SERVING

CALORIES:
1085

TOTAL FAT:
72 G

CARBS:
84 G

FIBER:
17 G

PROTEIN:
32 G

CALCIUM:
89 MG

VITAMIN D:
0 MCG

VITAMIN B12:
19 MCG

IRON:
6 MG

ZINC:
8 MG

Queso

The first time I shared this recipe with my husband, he was skeptical. He considers himself a nacho aficionado and is very picky about the "fake cheese sauce" I use. He was blown away by how creamy, thick, and cheesy this sauce is. This recipe is perfect in nachos, baked tacos, enchiladas, Tofu Huevos Rancheros (page 39), and Breakfast Burritos (page 43).

2 cups peeled and roughly chopped yellow potatoes
1 cup peeled and roughly chopped carrot
½ cup water
⅓ cup extra-virgin olive oil
1 tablespoon lemon juice
½ cup nutritional yeast

¼ teaspoon garlic powder
¼ teaspoon onion powder
1 teaspoon salt
¼ teaspoon cayenne pepper or red pepper flakes
3 tablespoons pickled jalapeños with liquid, divided

1. Bring a large pot of water to a boil and cook the potatoes and carrots until soft. Once done, drain and discard liquid.

2. In a blender or food processor, combine the water, olive oil, lemon juice, nutritional yeast, garlic powder, onion powder, salt, cayenne pepper, 2 tablespoons of pickled jalapeños, and add the potatoes and carrots. Blend until creamy.

3. Pour into a medium serving bowl and top with the remaining 1 tablespoon of jalapeños and serve. If storing, refrigerate leftovers in an airtight container for up to 5 days.

VARIATION TIP: If you can't find pickled jalapeños in your local grocer's Mexican section, you can use fresh jalapeños instead. Just remove the seeds and white rib first. If you want to add a smoky flavor to your queso, swap the cayenne for chipotle chili powder.

Vegan Caesar Dressing

MAKES
1 CUP

PREP TIME
5 MINUTES

I love Caesar salad, and I missed it when I adopted a plant-based lifestyle. I was so excited to find vegan Caesar dressing options at a specialty food shop, but when I tried them, only one (very expensive) option closely matched the taste of non-vegan Caesar dressing. I set out to make my own more affordable version. The base for this dressing is my Easy 4-Ingredient Vegan Mayonnaise (page 21). Add a few simple household staple ingredients, mix, and ta-da! You've got Caesar dressing.

½ cup Easy 4-Ingredient Vegan
   Mayonnaise (page 21)
1 tablespoon Dijon mustard
1 tablespoon soy sauce
1 tablespoon extra-virgin olive oil
¼ teaspoon white vinegar

1 tablespoon maple syrup
1 garlic clove, minced
2 tablespoons lemon juice
2 tablespoons nutritional yeast
2 teaspoons capers, drained

1. Prepare the Easy 4-Ingredient Vegan Mayonnaise.

2. Add the mayonnaise, mustard, soy sauce, olive oil, white vinegar, maple syrup, garlic, lemon juice, nutritional yeast, and capers to a blender and process until creamy. If storing, refrigerate for up to 5 days in an airtight container.

STRETCH TIP: Capers add a salty, pickled quality to this dressing, so it's worth picking up a small jar. They are also wonderful tossed in salads or with Garlic and Dill Sunflower Seed Cream Cheese (page 67). If you aren't a fan of capers, you can use green olives or fresh thyme in this recipe instead.

PER SERVING

CALORIES:
742

TOTAL FAT:
70 G

CARBS:
23 G

FIBER:
3 G

PROTEIN:
10 G

CALCIUM:
52 MG

VITAMIN D:
0 MCG

VITAMIN B12:
5 MCG

IRON:
2 MG

ZINC:
3 MG

Lemon Tahini Vinaigrette

MAKES
1 CUP

PREP TIME
3 MINUTES

PER SERVING

CALORIES:
1243

TOTAL FAT:
113 G

CARBS:
48 G

FIBER:
11 G

PROTEIN:
24 G

CALCIUM:
409 MG

VITAMIN D:
0 MCG

VITAMIN B12:
5 MCG

IRON:
9 MG

ZINC:
6 MG

I love the flavor combination of sesame and lemon. Sesame is so rich and nutty (although nut-free), and lemon has a wonderful bright flavor. This recipe uses tahini, which is made of ground sesame seeds. I use this dressing on salads, in bowls, and with falafel, but it shines when served with recipes that use chickpeas, like Chickpea Cauliflower Burgers (page 75) or Bulgur and Chickpea Tabbouleh (page 131).

⅓ cup tahini

⅓ cup water

¼ cup, plus 1 tablespoon freshly squeezed lemon juice

2 garlic cloves, chopped

¾ teaspoon salt

In a blender or food processor, combine the tahini, water, lemon juice, garlic cloves, and salt. Process until smooth. If storing, refrigerate in an airtight container for up to 5 days.

TECHNIQUE TIP: Always stir your tahini well before adding it to any recipe. Because tahini is all natural (it's ground sesame seeds), the solids and oils separate when it sits. Stirring well before use ensures you'll get the right flavor and texture in your dish.

Mushroom Gravy

MAKES
2 CUPS

PREP TIME
10 MINUTES

COOK TIME
10 MINUTES

This dark, rich gravy has Thanksgiving written all over it. It tastes like the gravy my grandmother used to spend hours making, but this one is quick. I use this gravy on Roasted Vegetable Pot Pie (page 119) or alongside Garlic Chive Red Mashed Potatoes (page 162). Or, you can eat it plain, straight from the spoon—I won't tell anyone!

¼ cup vegan butter

1 large onion, diced

8 ounces cremini mushrooms, thinly sliced

1 garlic clove, minced

¼ cup all-purpose flour

2½ cups vegetable broth, divided

2 tablespoons soy sauce

1 teaspoon dried oregano

1 teaspoon dried basil

½ teaspoon dried thyme

¼ teaspoon salt

½ teaspoon ground black pepper

PER SERVING

CALORIES:
679

TOTAL FAT:
46 G

CARBS:
56 G

FIBER:
8 G

PROTEIN:
16 G

CALCIUM:
153 MG

VITAMIN D:
7 MCG

VITAMIN B12:
0 MCG

IRON:
5 MG

ZINC:
3 MG

1. In a deep skillet, melt the vegan butter over medium heat. Add the onion and sauté until translucent, about 5 minutes. Add the mushrooms and continue to cook until soft and browned. Add the garlic and cook for 1 minute.

2. In a large measuring glass, combine the flour and ½ cup of vegetable broth to form a paste. Add the remaining 2 cups of broth and whisk until no lumps remain.

3. Add the broth and flour mixture to the skillet with the mushrooms and onion and whisk to combine. Add the soy sauce, oregano, basil, thyme, salt, and pepper. Stir well.

4. Bring to a boil, stirring constantly, and let the gravy cook at a boil for a few minutes until thickened. Remove from heat and adjust salt and pepper as needed. If storing, refrigerate for up to 2 days in an airtight container.

TECHNIQUE TIP: Mushrooms are very spongelike in their ability to absorb water, but too much water can dilute their flavor and keep them from caramelizing when cooked. Never wash mushrooms before using them. Use a damp paper towel to gently brush away any excess dirt before using.

Breakfast Burritos, 43

3

Tofu, Tempeh, and Soy

Tofu Scramble

MAKES
4 CUPS

PREP TIME
10 MINUTES

COOK TIME
15 MINUTES

PER SERVING

CALORIES:
258

TOTAL FAT:
16 G

CARBS:
10 G

FIBER:
3 G

PROTEIN:
23 G

CALCIUM:
505 MG

VITAMIN D:
2 MCG

VITAMIN B12:
2 MCG

IRON:
5 MG

ZINC:
3 MG

It took me a really long time to find an egg substitute that I loved enough to share. I tried so many variations before I came up with this recipe, which is reminiscent of traditional scrambled eggs. I'm proud of this recipe because it uses everyday ingredients that are likely already in your pantry or refrigerator (or else at your local grocery store), so there's no searching for obscure spices or expensive egg substitutes.

2 tablespoons extra-virgin olive oil
1 medium onion, diced
1 cup sliced mushrooms
2 garlic cloves, minced
1 cup fresh baby spinach leaves
1 cup grape tomatoes, halved
3 tablespoons soy sauce
1½ blocks extra-firm tofu, crumbled

¼ cup nutritional yeast
½ teaspoon turmeric
Water, to loosen scramble
   (optional)
Salt and pepper, to taste
½ cup vegan Cheddar-style shreds
   (optional)

1. Heat the oil in a large, deep skillet over medium-high heat. Add the onion and mushrooms, and sauté until the onion is translucent and mushrooms are slightly golden, about 5 minutes. Add the garlic and cook for 1 minute.

2. Add the spinach and tomatoes and cook until wilted and soft. Add the soy sauce and stir to combine.

3. Add the tofu, nutritional yeast, and turmeric. Mix well to combine and cook for about 5 minutes, or until the tofu is warmed through completely. If the scramble is dry, add 2 tablespoons of water to loosen it.

4. Season with salt and pepper and mix in the vegan Cheddar shreds. Stir until melted and serve immediately.

VARIATION TIP: This recipe is a great base for any type of scramble. For a plain scramble, leave out the veggies. To change it up, swap in different vegetables, or add Smoky Tofu "Bacon" (page 18) for a "bacon and egg" scramble and use it as a filling for vegan quiches, breakfast burritos, and wraps.

Tofu Huevos Rancheros

This recipe highlights the versatility of my Tofu Scramble (page 38). In this dish, I omit the spinach and mushrooms and use a basic tofu scramble before ramping it up with tomatoes, black beans, Pico de Gallo (page 23), avocado, and jalapeños. If I have enchilada or other hot sauce on hand, I sometimes drizzle it on top to add spice. I use flour tortillas here because they're convenient and versatile, but you can use corn tortillas instead.

For the Tofu Scramble

2 tablespoons extra-virgin olive oil

1 medium onion, diced

2 garlic cloves, minced

3 tablespoons soy sauce

1½ blocks extra-firm tofu, crumbled

¼ cup nutritional yeast

½ teaspoon turmeric

Water, to loosen scramble (optional)

Salt and pepper, to taste

½ cup vegan Cheddar-style shreds (optional)

For the Huevos Rancheros

¼ cup fresh salsa or Pico de Gallo (page 23)

1 cup canned black beans, drained and rinsed

4 large flour tortillas, warmed

2 ripe avocados, pitted and cubed

1 jalapeño, sliced into rounds (optional)

Hot sauce, to taste (optional)

TO MAKE THE TOFU SCRAMBLE

1. Heat the oil in a large, deep skillet over medium-high heat. Add the onions and sauté until translucent, about 5 minutes. Add the garlic and cook for one minute. Add the soy sauce and stir to combine.

2. Add the crumbled tofu, nutritional yeast, and turmeric. Mix well to combine and cook for about 5 minutes, or until the tofu is warmed through completely. (If the scramble is dry, add 2 tablespoons of water to loosen it.)

3. Season with salt and pepper and mix in the vegan Cheddar shreds. Stir until melted.

CONTINUED >

SERVES	4
PREP TIME	15 MINUTES
COOK TIME	15 MINUTES

PER SERVING

CALORIES: 781

TOTAL FAT: 51 G

CARBS: 29 G

FIBER: 8 G

PROTEIN: 64 G

CALCIUM: 1337 MG

VITAMIN D: 0 MCG

VITAMIN B12: 10 MCG

IRON: 13 MG

ZINC: 9 MG

Tofu Huevos Rancheros, CONTINUED

TO MAKE THE HUEVOS RANCHEROS

1. Prepare the Pico de Gallo salsa, if using.

2. Add the black beans to the skillet with the tofu scramble and stir to warm through.

3. In a separate medium skillet (or in the oven), warm the flour tortillas. Remove them from the skillet and place them on plates.

4. Add about 1 cup of tofu scramble and 1 tablespoon each of salsa and avocados to each tortilla. Top with jalapeños and sauce, if using, and serve immediately.

VARIATION TIP: Huevos Rancheros are usually served with refried pinto beans; if you're so inclined, you can use a can of them in place of the black beans in this recipe.

Broccoli Cheddar Quiche

SERVES
4 TO 6

PREP TIME
20 MINUTES

COOK TIME
30 MINUTES

This is a showstopping brunch dish. It looks like a full day's work, but in reality, it comes together in under an hour. You can use this recipe for any type of quiche. I've included my recipe for a homemade no-fail pie crust as the base of this quiche. It's simple and deliciously flaky. If you're short on time, or gluten-free, use a frozen deep-dish pie shell.

PER SERVING

CALORIES:
320

TOTAL FAT:
17 G

CARBS:
31 G

FIBER:
4 G

PROTEIN:
11 G

CALCIUM:
373 MG

VITAMIN D:
0 MCG

VITAMIN B12:
1 MCG

IRON:
3 MG

ZINC:
1 MG

For the crust

1½ cups all-purpose flour

½ teaspoon salt

½ cup chilled vegan butter

3 to 4 tablespoons cold water

For the quiche

2 to 3 cups plain Tofu Scramble (without veggies—see variation tip on page 38)

2 cups thawed and chopped frozen broccoli florets

2 cups vegan Cheddar-style shreds, divided

TO MAKE THE CRUST

1. Preheat the oven to 375°F.

2. In a large bowl, sift together the flour and salt. Add the cold butter and, using a pastry cutter or two knives, cut the butter into the flour until the butter is the size of small peas.

3. Add 2 tablespoons of cold water and mix to form a dough. If necessary, add more water, 1 tablespoon at a time, to moisten the dough. Roll into a ball.

4. On a floured surface, roll the dough into a circle about ¾ to 1 inch thick. Transfer to a 9-inch pie dish, gently pressing the sides and bottom down. Trim excess dough from the edges.

5. Using a fork, poke holes all over the bottom and sides of the crust to keep it from rising while baking. Place in the preheated oven and prebake for 10 to 12 minutes or until very lightly golden. Remove from the oven and set aside.

CONTINUED >

Broccoli Cheddar Quiche, CONTINUED

TO MAKE THE QUICHE

1. While the crust is baking, prepare the Tofu Scramble. Stir in the broccoli and 1 cup of the vegan Cheddar shreds.

2. Transfer the tofu scramble filling to the pie crust and top with the remaining 1 cup of Cheddar shreds.

3. Bake at 375°F for 10 minutes or until the crust edges are golden and the Cheddar is melted. Allow to cool at least 10 minutes before serving. Refrigerate leftovers.

PREP TIP: Make this dish a day in advance and refrigerate (or freeze) it until needed. Complete all steps except for baking, and bake just before serving time. If baking from frozen, bake at 375°F for 45 to 60 minutes.

Breakfast Burritos

I make a huge batch of these over the weekend and eat them for breakfast all week. You'll need to make a few things ahead of time for this recipe: Tofu Scramble (page 38), Vegan Cheddar Cheese Sauce (page 25), and Tofu Chorizo Crumble (page 16). For a less spicy version, swap the Tofu Chorizo Crumble for Meaty Tofu Crumble (page 17).

MAKES
5 TO 7 LARGE BURRITOS

PREP TIME
10 MINUTES

COOK TIME
20 MINUTES

PER SERVING

CALORIES:
660

TOTAL FAT:
36 G

CARBS:
68 G

FIBER:
15 G

PROTEIN:
32 G

CALCIUM:
752 MG

VITAMIN D:
30 MCG

VITAMIN B12:
2 MCG

IRON:
8 MG

ZINC:
2 MG

For the crispy potatoes

3 tablespoons extra-virgin olive oil
1 medium onion, diced
4 to 5 yellow potatoes, cut into ½-inch dice
2 garlic cloves, finely chopped
Salt and pepper, to taste

For the burritos

4 cups Tofu Scramble (page 38), divided
3 cups (1½ batches) Tofu Chorizo Crumble (page 16), divided
1 cup Vegan Cheddar Cheese Sauce (page 25), divided
8 large flour tortillas

TO MAKE THE CRISPY POTATOES

In a wide pan, heat the oil over medium-high heat. Add the onion and cook until translucent, about 5 minutes. Add the potatoes and cook until they are crispy on the outside and soft inside, about 15 minutes. Add the garlic and cook for one minute. Season with salt and pepper.

TO MAKE THE BURRITOS

1. Prepare the Tofu Scramble, Tofu Chorizo Crumble, and Vegan Cheddar Cheese Sauce.

2. Lay the tortillas out flat, one at a time. Place 2 tablespoons each of the Tofu Scramble, Tofu Chorizo Crumble, and crispy potatoes in a line down the center of each tortilla. Top with 1 to 2 tablespoons of Vegan Cheddar Cheese Sauce.

3. Fold in the sides of each burrito until they meet in the middle; then fold the bottom up, tucking it under as you roll toward the top of the burrito.

STRETCH TIP: These freeze well, so I often use smaller flour tortillas and make a big batch of mini breakfast burritos. Warm one up in the microwave for 1 to 2 minutes for a quick, on-the-go breakfast.

Tempeh Breakfast Hash

SERVES
4

PREP TIME
15 MINUTES

COOK TIME
30 MINUTES

PER SERVING

CALORIES:
724

TOTAL FAT:
39 G

CARBS:
71 G

FIBER:
15 G

PROTEIN:
37 G

CALCIUM:
785 MG

VITAMIN D:
30 MCG

VITAMIN B12:
2 MCG

IRON:
9 MG

ZINC:
2 MG

I often make breakfast hash on Saturday mornings after I find my vegetable crisper drawer full of half-used vegetables from earlier in the week. Breakfast hash is a great way to use up leftovers and turn them into a delicious, filling breakfast. While your hash is cooking, whip up a quick batch of Smoky Tempeh "Bacon" (see variation tip on page 18) to give this recipe a "meaty" boost—and some extra protein.

6 strips Smoky Tempeh "Bacon," diced (page 18)

½ cup Vegan Cheddar Cheese Sauce, warmed (page 25)

3 tablespoons extra-virgin olive oil

1 medium onion, diced

4 to 5 yellow potatoes, cut into ½-inch dice

3 garlic cloves, minced

1 red bell pepper, diced

1 green bell pepper, diced

½ teaspoon salt

½ teaspoon ground black pepper

3 scallions, finely chopped

Hot sauce (optional)

1. Prepare the diced Smoky Tempeh "Bacon" and Vegan Cheddar Cheese Sauce.

2. In a deep skillet, heat the oil over medium-high heat. Add the onion and sauté for about 5 minutes or until the onion is translucent but not browned. Add the potatoes and garlic and toss with the onions. Cook until the potatoes are soft and golden on the outside, about 15 minutes.

3. Add the bell peppers and cook for 5 minutes. Season with salt and pepper.

4. Add the tempeh "bacon" to the skillet. Toss to combine and cook until it is warmed through.

5. Transfer the hash to bowls and top with vegan cheese sauce, scallions, and hot sauce, if using, to taste.

STRETCH TIP: Turn leftovers of this dish into a quick, on-the-go weekday morning breakfast (and use up any leftover tortillas) by making breakfast hash burritos. Stash them in the freezer and, when ready, microwave them for 1 to 2 minutes.

Tempeh "Chicken" Salad Sandwiches

SERVES
4 TO 6

PREP TIME
10 MINUTES

I was recently at a gourmet grocery store and noticed a vegan "chicken" salad sandwich made with tempeh. Intrigued, I purchased it and ate it on the drive home. It was delicious, bright, and flavorful—but it was also expensive. On my way home, I stopped at my regular grocery store and picked up some ingredients to try to re-create it, and I think I did it justice. This recipe can also be served on crackers or on top of mixed greens in a salad.

PER SERVING

CALORIES:
244

TOTAL FAT:
23 G

CARBS:
5 G

FIBER:
2 G

PROTEIN:
8 G

CALCIUM:
53 MG

VITAMIN D:
0 MCG

VITAMIN B12:
0 MCG

IRON:
1 MG

ZINC:
1 MG

For the tempeh salad

1 cup plus 2 tablespoons Easy 4-Ingredient Vegan Mayonnaise (page 21)
1 (8-ounce) package plain tempeh
½ red bell pepper, diced
1 celery stalk, diced
2 scallions, finely chopped (whites and greens)
1 tablespoon lemon juice

1 teaspoon soy sauce
1 tablespoon finely chopped fresh dill
½ teaspoon salt
½ teaspoon ground black pepper

For the sandwiches

4 to 6 slices whole grain bread
4 to 6 iceberg or butter lettuce leaves

TO MAKE THE TEMPEH SALAD

1. Prepare Easy 4-Ingredient Vegan Mayonnaise.

2. In a large bowl, crumble the tempeh. Add 1 cup of mayonnaise, the bell pepper, celery, scallions, lemon juice, soy sauce, dill, salt, and pepper. Mix thoroughly. Add more salt and pepper to taste.

TO MAKE THE SANDWICHES

Use the remaining 2 tablespoons of mayonnaise to spread on each slice of bread. Assemble each sandwich with a slice of lettuce and a heaping scoop of tempeh salad. Refrigerate leftovers.

VARIATION TIP: If you don't have fresh dill on hand, dried will work as well—use half the amount, as dried dill has a stronger flavor.

Tempeh BLT

SERVES
4

PREP TIME
5 MINUTES

COOK TIME
10 MINUTES

PER SERVING

CALORIES:
259

TOTAL FAT:
14 G

CARBS:
23 G

FIBER:
6 G

PROTEIN:
15 G

CALCIUM:
70 MG

VITAMIN D:
0 MCG

VITAMIN B12:
0 MCG

IRON:
2 MG

ZINC:
1 MG

I'm a sandwich person, and this is one of my favorites. It's quick to make, and it's hearty and satisfying. I like to change up the flavors by adding avocado, roasted red bell peppers, or a chopped up sun-dried tomato. If you're making my Easy 4-Ingredient Vegan Mayonnaise for this sandwich, consider adding some heat by using one of the alternate recipes I included in the variation tip on page 21.

For the tempeh

2 tablespoons tamari or dark
  soy sauce
1 tablespoon maple syrup
1 teaspoon apple cider vinegar
3 drops liquid smoke
1 tablespoon extra-virgin olive oil
1 (8-ounce) block tempeh, cut into
  ¼-inch strips

For the sandwiches

2 tablespoons Easy 4-Ingredient
  Vegan Mayonnaise (page 21)
4 to 8 slices whole grain
  bread, toasted
4 to 6 iceberg or butter
  lettuce leaves
1 large tomato, sliced

TO MAKE THE TEMPEH

1. Make a marinade for the tempeh: In a small bowl, combine the tamari, maple syrup, vinegar, and liquid smoke.

2. In a large, deep skillet, heat the olive oil over medium-high. When hot, add the tempeh slices and sauté until golden brown on each side.

3. Add the marinade to the pan and continue to cook until almost all the liquid is gone and the tempeh strips are sticky and caramelized, about 3 minutes.

TO MAKE THE SANDWICHES

1. Prepare Easy 4-Ingredient Vegan Mayonnaise.

2. Spread the mayonnaise on each slice of bread. Layer lettuce, tomato, and tempeh on one side. Top with a second slice of bread.

SUBSTITUTION TIP: Gluten-free? Turn this BLT sandwich into a fabulous BLT salad instead. Skip the bread and serve over 2 cups of chopped iceberg lettuce.

Tofu Egg Salad Sandwiches

SERVES
4 TO 6

PREP TIME
10 MINUTES

My stepdad used to pack my school lunches, and he had a tried-and-true egg salad sandwich recipe that was a staple in my house. I'm convinced to this day that his is *the best egg salad ever*. He passed the recipe down to me when I was a teenager, and I used it as my inspiration for this vegan version. He passed away a few years ago, but if he were here, I know he'd say I did him proud with this one.

PER SERVING

CALORIES:
93

TOTAL FAT:
8 G

CARBS:
2 G

FIBER:
1 G

PROTEIN:
6 G

CALCIUM:
166 MG

VITAMIN D:
0 MCG

VITAMIN B12:
0 MCG

IRON:
1 MG

ZINC:
1 MG

For the tofu egg salad

5 to 6 tablespoons Easy 4-Ingredient Vegan Mayonnaise (page 21), divided

1 (12-ounce) block extra-firm tofu, drained and pressed

2 scallions, sliced in half lengthwise, then finely chopped

2 teaspoons spicy brown or yellow mustard

2 teaspoons sweet relish

¼ teaspoon kosher salt

1 teaspoon ground black pepper

For the sandwiches

4 to 8 slices whole grain bread

4 to 6 iceberg or butter lettuce leaves

1 large tomato, sliced

TO MAKE THE TOFU EGG SALAD

1. Prepare Easy 4-Ingredient Vegan Mayonnaise.

2. Using the large-grate side of a box grater, grate the tofu into a large bowl.

3. Add the scallions, 3 tablespoons of mayonnaise (add more if you want a wetter consistency), mustard, relish, salt, and pepper. Mix well. Taste and adjust seasoning.

TO MAKE THE SANDWICHES

Spread the remaining 2 tablespoons of mayonnaise on each slice of bread. Assemble each sandwich with a slice of lettuce, tomato, and a heaping scoop of tofu egg salad. Refrigerate leftovers.

TECHNIQUE TIP: If you don't have a box grater, don't worry. You can get a great texture for this salad by crumbling your tofu with a potato masher.

Crispy Buffalo Tofu Wrap

SERVES
4

PREP TIME
10 MINUTES

COOK TIME
10 MINUTES

PER SERVING

CALORIES:
419

TOTAL FAT:
32 G

CARBS:
24 G

FIBER:
2 G

PROTEIN:
12 G

CALCIUM:
255 MG

VITAMIN D:
0 MCG

VITAMIN B12:
0 MCG

IRON:
4 MG

ZINC:
1 MG

This wrap is fun to make when you're having friends over to watch a game, or as part of a sandwich platter. I love the contrast of the heat from the sauce, the bright, acidic bite of the pickles, and the coolness of the dressing. Typically, Buffalo-style is served with a side of ranch or blue cheese dressing, but in a pinch, my Vegan Caesar Dressing (page 33) works well, too.

For the Buffalo tofu

1 (12-ounce) block extra-firm tofu, drained, pressed, and cut into cubes

2 tablespoons cornstarch

⅓ cup vegan butter, melted

½ cup Buffalo wing hot sauce, such as Frank's Red Hot

2 tablespoons extra-virgin olive oil

For the wraps

1 tablespoon Vegan Caesar Dressing (page 33)

4 to 6 iceberg or butter lettuce leaves

4 large flour tortillas

½ cup sliced bread-and-butter pickles

TO MAKE THE BUFFALO TOFU

1. Toss the tofu in a bowl with the cornstarch. Stir to coat. Set aside.

2. In a small bowl, combine the melted butter and hot sauce. Stir until incorporated and set aside.

3. In a large, deep skillet, heat the oil on medium-high heat. When the oil is hot, add the tofu. Cook on all sides for 6 to 8 minutes, stirring frequently until the tofu is golden and crisp and the oil is absorbed.

4. Once the tofu is crispy, pour the hot sauce mix into the pan and swirl to coat the tofu. Transfer the tofu to a bowl.

TO MAKE THE WRAPS

1. Prepare the Vegan Caesar Dressing.

2. Place lettuce on each tortilla. Top with 2 tablespoons of Buffalo tofu, pickles, and Caesar dressing. Fold into wraps and serve immediately.

TECHNIQUE TIP: If you want to avoid using oil, you can bake the tofu in the oven instead. Place the tofu cubes on a large, parchment-lined rimmed baking sheet in a single layer. Bake at 400°F for 15 to 20 minutes or until golden.

Spicy Tofu "Crab" Salad in a Pita

SERVES
4

PREP TIME
10 MINUTES

There used to be a deli my family ate at often, and I almost always ordered the Pita Pocket Trio: three half-pitas stuffed with egg, tuna, and crab salads. I always saved the crab one for last. I created this vegan "crab" salad in memory of my old deli favorite. The shredded tofu mimics the texture of a shredded crab salad. It's a cross between old-fashioned crab salad and the filling in a spicy crab sushi roll—only vegan.

PER SERVING

CALORIES:
623

TOTAL FAT:
35 G

CARBS:
50 G

FIBER:
11 G

PROTEIN:
43 G

CALCIUM:
1059 MG

VITAMIN D:
0 MCG

VITAMIN B12:
0 MCG

IRON:
9 MG

ZINC:
4 MG

For the tofu "crab" salad

2 tablespoons Easy 4-Ingredient Vegan Mayonnaise (page 21)

1 (12-ounce) block extra-firm tofu, drained and pressed

½ teaspoon Old Bay seasoning

2 scallions, finely chopped

¼ to ½ teaspoon sriracha, to taste

For the pita pockets

2 pita pockets, cut in half

4 iceberg or butter lettuce leaves

TO MAKE THE TOFU "CRAB" SALAD

1. Prepare the Easy 4-Ingredient Vegan Mayonnaise.

2. Using the large-grate side of a box grater, grate the tofu into shreds and put into a bowl.

3. Add the vegan mayonnaise, Old Bay seasoning, scallions, and sriracha to the tofu. Mix well to combine. Taste and adjust the seasoning.

TO MAKE THE PITA POCKETS

Open the pita pocket halves and line them with lettuce. Add a scoop of Tofu "Crab" Salad to each pocket.

VARIATION TIP: If you don't have Old Bay seasoning on hand, you can make your own by combining 2 tablespoons of celery salt, ¼ teaspoon of paprika, and ⅛ teaspoon each of black pepper, cayenne pepper, ground mustard, and ground nutmeg.

Crunchy Tofu Taco Salad

SERVES
8

PREP TIME
15 MINUTES

PER SERVING

CALORIES:
630

TOTAL FAT:
35 G

CARBS:
67 G

FIBER:
18 G

PROTEIN:
18 G

CALCIUM:
260 MG

VITAMIN D:
3 CG

VITAMIN B12:
1 MCG

IRON:
6 MG

ZINC:
3 MG

This salad is great at parties, picnics, or potlucks, or for a take-to-work lunch. Tofu Chorizo Crumble (page 16) makes this dish feel Tex-Mex. To keep the salad from getting soggy and brown, refrigerate the components separately and combine them for each serving. I prefer to use a store-bought mild salsa in this recipe because it has more liquid, which adds moisture.

2 cups (1 batch) Tofu Chorizo Crumble, cooled (page 16)

1½ cups Vegan Caesar Dressing (page 33)

1 large iceberg lettuce, shredded

2 cups tortilla chips, coarsely crushed

1 (16-ounce) can kidneys beans, drained and rinsed

1 (16-ounce) can black beans, drained and rinsed

4 cups halved grape tomatoes

3 scallions, finely chopped

1 cup salsa

1 cup vegan Cheddar-style shreds

2 avocados, pitted and cubed

1 cup diced black olives

¼ cup thinly sliced jalapeños

1. Prepare Tofu Chorizo Crumble and Vegan Caesar Dressing.

2. In a large bowl, layer the lettuce, tofu chorizo crumble, tortilla chips, kidney beans, black beans, tomatoes, and scallions.

3. In a large measuring glass, combine the Caesar dressing and salsa. Pour the mixture over the salad and toss to combine.

4. Top with Cheddar shreds, avocado, olives, and jalapeños. Serve immediately and refrigerate leftovers.

TECHNIQUE TIP: Most grocery stores sell pre-shredded lettuce, but it's more expensive than buying a head and shredding it yourself. To shred a head of iceberg lettuce, slice the head into quarters and shred it with a box grater. You can do this even faster with a food processor—simply attach the large slicing blade and feed the quarters through.

Tofu Chorizo Enchiladas

SERVES
4 TO 6

PREP TIME
20 MINUTES

COOK TIME
40 MINUTES

My eldest daughter asks for enchiladas at least once a week. We've created several different versions of this dish using whatever we have in the kitchen. I get asked to make this recipe all the time—my dad once visited on the condition that I made this for dinner when he arrived. I think a 1,400-mile trip warrants a tray of enchiladas, don't you?

1 recipe (2 cups) Tofu Chorizo Crumble (page 16)

2 cups Stovetop Enchilada Sauce (page 26)

1½ cups Vegan Cheddar Cheese Sauce (page 25)

Roasted Garlic Guacamole (page 22), as topping (optional)

3 tablespoons extra-virgin olive oil, divided

1 medium onion, diced

1 garlic clove, minced

8 large flour tortillas

¼ cup sliced jalapeños

Vegan sour cream, as topping (optional)

1. Prepare Tofu Chorizo Crumble, Stovetop Enchilada Sauce, Vegan Cheddar Cheese Sauce, and Roasted Garlic Guacamole, if using.

2. In a deep skillet, heat 2 tablespoon of olive oil over medium-high heat. Sauté the onion until soft and lightly browned. Add the garlic and cook for 1 minute. Add the tofu chorizo to the pan and stir to combine.

3. Grease a 9-inch by 11-inch baking dish with the remaining 1 tablespoon of olive oil. Preheat the oven to 375°F.

4. Fill a tortilla with 3 tablespoons of tofu chorizo, 1 tablespoon of enchilada sauce, and 1 tablespoon of Vegan Cheddar Cheese Sauce. Fold in the sides of the tortilla until they almost meet in the middle, then fold up the bottom, tucking it in as you roll toward the top of the tortilla. Place in the greased baking dish and repeat with all tortillas.

5. Ladle the remaining enchilada and cheese sauces over the tortillas and top with jalapeños. Bake for 15 minutes or until the sauces are bubbling, and serve immediately with guacamole and sour cream, if using. Refrigerate leftovers for up to 3 days.

PREP TIP: Got a busy week ahead? Prep this dish (up to step 5) on the weekend, and stash in the fridge until needed. When ready to eat, add the sauces and jalapeños on top and bake.

PER SERVING

CALORIES:
332

TOTAL FAT:
16 G

CARBS:
42 G

FIBER:
8 G

PROTEIN:
10 G

CALCIUM:
129 MG

VITAMIN D:
0 MCG

VITAMIN B12:
0 MCG

IRON:
2 MG

ZINC:
1 MG

Spicy Ginger Tofu

SERVES
4

PREP TIME
10 MINUTES

COOK TIME
10 MINUTES

PER SERVING

CALORIES:
398

TOTAL FAT:
28 G

CARBS:
21 G

FIBER:
3 G

PROTEIN:
22 G

CALCIUM:
592 MG

VITAMIN D:
0 MCG

VITAMIN B12:
0 MCG

IRON:
6 MG

ZINC:
3 MG

This is a fantastic weeknight dinner. In the time it takes to make a pot of rice, you can have this entire dish cooked and ready to go. Sometimes, I like to make the sauce a day or two ahead and stash it in the fridge until I need it. It's particularly helpful when I have a super-busy week coming up and I need to meal plan and prep ahead of time. If you'd like, you could swap the tahini in this dish for creamy peanut butter. Both have deep, nutty flavors, but tahini has the bonus of being nut-free.

¼ cup, plus 2 tablespoons tahini

¼ cup soy sauce

2 tablespoons maple syrup, divided

1 tablespoon grated fresh ginger

2 tablespoons lime juice

2 (12-ounce) blocks extra-firm tofu, drained and pressed, cut into cubes

3 tablespoons cornstarch

2 tablespoons extra-virgin olive oil

Cooked rice or noodles, for serving

1. Make the ginger sauce: In a jar with a tight-fitting lid, combine the tahini, soy sauce, maple syrup, ginger, and lime juice. Shake well to mix thoroughly.

2. In a medium bowl, combine the tofu and cornstarch. Toss to coat.

3. Heat the oil in a large skillet over medium-high heat. Add the tofu and cook on all sides, tossing frequently, until the tofu is golden and crispy and the oil is absorbed.

4. Pour the ginger sauce into the pan and toss with the tofu for 3 minutes to coat. Serve immediately over rice or noodles.

VARIATION TIP: This sauce also makes a great salad dressing. Add ¼ cup of olive oil to the jar of ginger sauce and whisk or shake thoroughly. Keep refrigerated and use it on any salad, shaking before each use.

Sweet and Spicy Crispy Tofu

SERVES
4

PREP TIME
10 MINUTES

COOK TIME
15 MINUTES

This recipe is inspired by one of my husband's old favorite dishes from a Chinese restaurant near our house—Crispy Beef. The sauce is sticky and sweet and has just enough heat to tickle your taste buds without over-powering them. To achieve the crispy edges on the tofu, I recommend you tear the tofu into pieces with your hands. The rough, uneven surface of the tofu helps the sauce to stick to more of the tofu and crisp up better.

PER SERVING

CALORIES:
534

TOTAL FAT:
22 G

CARBS:
53 G

FIBER:
7 G

PROTEIN:
32 G

CALCIUM:
551 MG

VITAMIN D:
0 MCG

VITAMIN B12:
0 MCG

IRON:
3 MG

ZINC:
0 MG

3 tablespoons extra-virgin olive oil, divided
½ teaspoon ginger, grated
4 garlic cloves, minced
½ cup soy sauce
¼ cup water
½ cup packed brown sugar
¼ to ½ teaspoon sriracha, to taste

2 (12-ounce) blocks extra-firm tofu, pressed to remove moisture and torn into bite-size pieces
⅓ cup cornstarch
½ large white onion, diced
1 green bell pepper, diced
2 scallions, finely chopped

1. Heat 1 tablespoon of olive oil in a small pan over medium-low heat. Add the ginger and garlic. Stir for 1 to 2 minutes, until warm and fragrant. Add the soy sauce, water, brown sugar, and sriracha, and bring to a boil. Allow the mixture to boil for 3 to 5 minutes or until slightly thickened, stirring occasionally. Set aside.

2. Add the torn tofu pieces to a large resealable plastic bag and add cornstarch. Shake to coat. Remove the tofu from the bag and set aside.

3. Place 1 tablespoon of olive oil in a large skillet or wok and heat over medium-high heat. Add the onion, bell pepper, and scallions. Cook until the bell pepper is soft and the onion is translucent.

4. Pour in the remaining 1 tablespoon of olive oil and add the tofu. Do not overcrowd the pan, and work in 2 batches if your pan isn't wide enough.

5. Cook the tofu, tossing frequently, until all sides are browned. Add the sauce to the pan and cook over medium-high heat until hot and bubbly, about 5 minutes. Serve immediately and refrigerate leftovers.

Sweet and Sour Tofu

SERVES
4

PREP TIME
10 MINUTES

COOK TIME
20 MINUTES

PER SERVING

CALORIES:
796

TOTAL FAT:
28 G

CARBS:
109 G

FIBER:
4 G

PROTEIN:
32 G

CALCIUM:
282 MG

VITAMIN D:
0 MCG

VITAMIN B12:
0 MCG

IRON:
5 MG

ZINC:
1 MG

I have a complicated relationship with sweet and sour sauce. I love the flavor, but it's usually made with pineapple, and I have a severe pineapple allergy. Fortunately, pineapple and orange juice are equal parts sweet, sour, and acidic. If you prefer pineapple, go ahead and use it instead.

½ cup ketchup

1 tablespoon soy sauce

¾ cup white vinegar

½ cup light brown sugar

½ cup granulated sugar

¾ cup orange juice

1 cup water, divided

¼ cup, plus 2 tablespoons cornstarch, divided

2 (12-ounce) blocks extra-firm tofu, drained, pressed to remove moisture, and torn into bite-size pieces

4 tablespoons extra-virgin olive oil, divided

1 medium onion, diced

1 green bell pepper, diced

2 cups cooked basmati or jasmine rice

1. In a medium saucepan, whisk the ketchup, soy sauce, vinegar, light brown sugar, granulated sugar, orange juice, and ¾ cup of water.

2. In a small bowl, combine the remaining ¼ cup of water and ¼ cup of cornstarch and mix until smooth. Add this mixture to the saucepan and stir until the sauce is thickened and glossy, about 5 minutes. Set aside.

3. In a medium bowl, combine the tofu with the remaining 2 tablespoons of cornstarch and toss to coat.

4. In a large, deep skillet, heat 2 tablespoons of olive oil over medium-high heat. Add the tofu and cook on all sides until the tofu is crispy and golden. Remove from the skillet and set aside.

5. Heat the remaining 2 tablespoons of olive oil in the same skillet over medium-high heat and add the onions. Cook for 5 to 7 minutes, until translucent and soft. Add the bell peppers and cook for 2 minutes or until slightly softened. Add the tofu and sauce to the skillet and toss to coat. Cook for 2 minutes or until the sauce starts to bubble. Remove and serve over rice.

VARIATION TIP: Swap the tofu for cauliflower. Toss the cauliflower florets in olive oil and bake at 400°F for 15 to 20 minutes until golden.

Sweet Chili Mango Tofu

SERVES
4

PREP TIME
15 MINUTES

COOK TIME
20 MINUTES

On Thursday nights, my friends and I would gather at my place and order Joy Thai for dinner. I always got my favorite: Mango Tofu. I've worked on this recreation for years, and I think it's a pretty close ode to an old favorite.

2 tablespoons Stir-Fry Sauce (page 28) or vegan Worcestershire sauce

3 cups frozen mango, thawed and divided

1 teaspoon sweet chili sauce

1 tablespoon vinegar (rice, apple cider, or white)

2 tablespoons soy sauce

1 tablespoon lime juice

1 tablespoon brown sugar

1 (2-inch) piece ginger, peeled and thinly sliced

3 garlic cloves, sliced

¼ teaspoon turmeric

4 tablespoons extra-virgin olive oil, divided

2 (12-ounce) blocks extra-firm tofu, drained, pressed, and cubed

1 medium onion, diced

1 red bell pepper, diced

Water, to thin sauce (optional)

½ cup whole cashews, for garnish (optional)

2 scallions, finely chopped, for garnish (optional)

PER SERVING

CALORIES:
445

TOTAL FAT:
24 G

CARBS:
37 G

FIBER:
4 G

PROTEIN:
23 G

CALCIUM:
336 MG

VITAMIN D:
0 MCG

VITAMIN B12:
0 MCG

IRON:
3 MG

ZINC:
0 MG

1. Prepare the Stif-Fry Sauce. Next, in a blender or food processor, combine 2 cups of the mango, the sweet chili sauce, vinegar, soy sauce, Stir-Fry Sauce, lime juice, brown sugar, ginger, garlic, and turmeric. Purée until smooth. The sauce may seem thick, but it will thin as it cooks. Set aside.

2. In a large, deep skillet, heat 2 tablespoons of oil over medium-high heat. Add the tofu and cook on all sides until golden, about 10 minutes. Remove from skillet and set aside.

3. Add the remaining 2 tablespoons of olive oil and the onions to the skillet and cook for 5 to 7 minutes, until the onions are trans-lucent and soft. Add the bell pepper and mango sauce. Bring to a gentle boil, then reduce to a simmer for 3 to 5 minutes. If the sauce is thick, add water 1 tablespoon at a time to thin it.

4. Return the tofu to the skillet and add the remaining 1 cup of mango. Stir to combine and cook until warm, about 3 minutes. Garnish with the cashews and scallions, if using.

Seasoned Breaded Tofu Cutlets with Linguini

SERVES
4

PREP TIME
10 MINUTES

COOK TIME
20 MINUTES

PER SERVING

CALORIES:
638

TOTAL FAT:
17 G

CARBS:
89 G

FIBER:
10 G

PROTEIN:
37 G

CALCIUM:
472 MG

VITAMIN D:
30 MCG

VITAMIN B12:
2 MCG

IRON:
8 MG

ZINC:
3 MG

This is a unique use for tofu and a great way to add some protein to pasta night. It's a relatively quick dish—I find I can get it seasoned and cooked in the time it takes to make a pot of pasta, which makes it a great weeknight dinner. I like using pizza seasoning for this because it combines ten different spices in one economical (and space-saving) bottle.

For the tofu cutlets

1 cup unsweetened soy or coconut milk

2 cups panko bread crumbs

3 tablespoons Italian or pizza seasoning

2 tablespoons nutritional yeast

½ teaspoon salt

½ teaspoon ground black pepper

2 (12-ounce) blocks extra-firm tofu, drained, pressed, and sliced in half lengthwise

For the linguini dish

1 (24-ounce) jar marinara sauce

1 (16-ounce) box linguini

TO MAKE THE TOFU CUTLETS

1. Preheat the oven to 400°F. Line a large rimmed baking sheet with parchment paper.

2. Prepare two shallow bowls. Add milk to the first bowl. In the second bowl, combine the panko, pizza seasoning, nutritional yeast, salt, and pepper. Stir until well mixed.

3. Working one at a time, dip each tofu cutlet into milk, then toss it into the seasoned panko bread crumbs. Transfer the cutlets to the prepared baking sheet.

4. Bake for 20 to 25 minutes, or until golden, flipping the tofu cutlets halfway through to ensure they brown on both sides.

TO MAKE THE LINGUINI DISH

1. While the tofu is cooking, gently heat the marinara sauce on the stove. Bring a pot of salted water to a boil and cook the linguini according to package directions.

2. Remove the tofu cutlets from the oven. Serve the cutlets on top of the linguini and drizzle with marinara sauce.

VARIATION TIP: These cutlets are extremely versatile. Try serving them with Garlic Chive Red Mashed Potatoes (page 162) and Mushroom Gravy (page 35) and some steamed green beans.

Cajun-Spiced Tofu Steaks

SERVES
4

PREP TIME
30 MINUTES

COOK TIME
10 MINUTES

PER SERVING

CALORIES:
352

TOTAL FAT:
26 G

CARBS:
8 G

FIBER:
2 G

PROTEIN:
22 G

CALCIUM:
331 MG

VITAMIN D:
0 MCG

VITAMIN B12:
1 MCG

IRON:
4 MG

ZINC:
0 MG

This is a vegan play on blackened chicken. The warm, spicy heat from Cajun-style seasoning adds a wonderful kick to tofu, which is the perfect canvas for bold flavor. The longer you marinate the tofu, the more intense the flavor. I like serving this on a hearty grain like farro or barley, a side of my White Garlic Dill Sauce (page 27), and a crisp salad to help cool things down.

For the Cajun-style marinade

2 teaspoons garlic powder

1 teaspoon onion powder

2½ teaspoons paprika

1¼ teaspoons oregano

2 teaspoons salt

1 teaspoon ground black pepper

1 teaspoon cayenne pepper

1¼ teaspoons dried thyme

¼ cup extra-virgin olive oil

For the tofu steaks

2 (12-ounce) blocks extra-firm tofu, drained, pressed, and sliced in half lengthwise into cutlets

¼ cup White Garlic Dill Sauce (page 27)

3 tablespoons olive oil

TO MAKE THE CAJUN-STYLE MARINADE

In a small bowl, mix the garlic powder, onion powder, paprika, oregano, salt, black pepper, cayenne pepper, thyme, and olive oil. Transfer to a large, shallow container and set aside.

TO MAKE THE TOFU STEAKS

1. Place the sliced tofu cutlets in the marinade, cover, and refrigerate for a minimum of 30 minutes or overnight.

2. While the tofu marinates, prepare the White Garlic Dill Sauce.

3. In a wide cast-iron or nonstick skillet, heat the oil over medium-high heat. Add the tofu cutlets, making sure not to overcrowd them. Cook until the tofu is browned and crispy on all sides.

4. Remove from the pan and serve with White Garlic Dill Sauce on their own or alongside your favorite grain.

PREP TIP: Prep the marinade, tofu, and dill sauce the night before and refrigerate overnight. You'll shorten your cook time on a busy weeknight.

BBQ Tempeh and Caramelized Onion Tavern Burgers

SERVES
4

PREP TIME
5 MINUTES

COOK TIME
10 MINUTES

This tavern burger is a fun, grown-up take on a sloppy joe, served as an intentionally messy sandwich on a bun with sautéed onions, pickles, ketchup, mustard, and cheese. For this vegan version, I like to combine tempeh and tofu to give the dish different textures. Feel free to make it with either all tempeh or all tofu—just don't forget the pickles.

4 cups (2 batches) Meaty Tofu Crumble (page 17)
1 cup Homemade BBQ Sauce (page 24)
1 cup Quick Caramelized Onions (page 19)
2 tablespoons extra-virgin olive oil

1 (8-ounce) package tempeh, crumbled
2 tablespoons ketchup
2 tablespoons yellow mustard
4 hamburger buns
½ cup bread-and-butter pickles

1. Prepare the Meaty Tofu Crumble, Homemade BBQ Sauce, and Quick Caramelized Onions.

2. In a deep skillet, heat the oil over medium-high heat. Crumble the tempeh into the pan and cook for 5 minutes to warm through.

3. Add the tofu crumble, BBQ sauce, ketchup, and mustard. Stir to combine. Cook until the mixture is warmed through, about 5 minutes.

4. Arrange the burger buns on a plate and scoop a hearty portion of the BBQ tempeh and tofu mixture on the bottom buns. Top with caramelized onions and pickles. Add the top bun to each.

PREP TIP: To make this an easy, 15-minute weeknight dinner, make the tofu crumble and the caramelized onions a day or two ahead and keep them refrigerated. If you don't have the time to make a batch of caramelized onions, simply sauté the onions in the pan before you add the tempeh and tofu and mix it all together.

PER SERVING

CALORIES:
861

TOTAL FAT:
46 G

CARBS:
78 G

FIBER:
14 G

PROTEIN:
41 G

CALCIUM:
558 MG

VITAMIN D:
0 MCG

VITAMIN B12:
0 MCG

IRON:
9 MG

ZINC:
2 MG

Soy Curl Shawarma Wrap

SERVES
3 TO 4

PREP TIME
15 MINUTES

COOK TIME
25 MINUTES

PER SERVING

CALORIES:
666

TOTAL FAT:
43 G

CARBS:
56 G

FIBER:
24 G

PROTEIN:
35 G

CALCIUM:
244 MG

VITAMIN D:
0 MCG

VITAMIN B12:
1 MCG

IRON:
10 MG

ZINC:
2 MG

Shawarma, which has its origins in Middle Eastern cooking, is slow-roasted marinated and spiced meat. To veganize chicken shawarma, I use Butler's Soy Curls, which are dried soy protein strips that when rehydrated and cooked, develop a chewy texture similar to chicken (they're available in many grocery stores and online). The shawarma spice mix in this recipe makes two batches, so save the rest to use next time you make this dish.

For the shawarma soy curls

1 (8-ounce) package dried Butler's Soy Curls

1 teaspoon water, reserved from soy curls

1 tablespoon ground coriander

½ teaspoon ground allspice

½ teaspoon ground cinnamon

½ teaspoon ground cumin

½ teaspoon garlic powder

½ teaspoon chili powder

¼ teaspoon ground ginger

¼ teaspoon turmeric

¼ teaspoon ground black pepper

1 tablespoon extra-virgin olive oil

For the wraps

1 cup Lemon Tahini Vinaigrette (page 34)

4 pitas or tortilla wraps

1 to 2 cups shredded iceberg lettuce

1 seedless cucumber, diced

2 cups grape tomatoes, halved

½ red onion, thinly sliced

TO MAKE THE SHAWARMA SOY CURLS

1. Rehydrate the soy curls by soaking them in a large bowl of water for 10 minutes. Strain, reserving 1 teaspoon of the soaking water.

2. Preheat your oven to 400°F. Line a large rimmed baking sheet with parchment paper.

3. While the soy curls rehydrate, make a shawarma spice mix. In a small bowl, combine the coriander, allspice, cinnamon, cumin, garlic powder, chili powder, ground ginger, turmeric, and black pepper.

4. In a large bowl, combine the spice mix, olive oil, and reserved water to form a paste. Add to the soy curls and toss until well coated.

5. Spread the soy curls on the parchment-lined baking sheet in an even layer and bake for 20 to 25 minutes, flipping halfway through. Cool slightly.

TO MAKE THE WRAPS

1. While the soy curls are cooking, prepare the Lemon Tahini Vinaigrette.

2. Layer the open wraps with lettuce, shawarma soy curls, cucumber, tomato, and onion. Drizzle with the vinaigrette. Fold the wraps and serve immediately. Refrigerate leftovers.

VARIATION TIP: If you don't have access to Butler's Soy Curls, use 1 (15-ounce) can of chickpeas, drained and rinsed, as a replacement filling for these wraps. Toss the chickpeas with the olive oil and shawarma spice mix, and roast them at 400°F for 20 to 25 minutes, stirring halfway through.

Lentil and Mushroom Sweet Potato Shepard's Pie, 77

4

Beans, Legumes, and Seeds

Chickpea Florentine Frittatas

SERVES
4

PREP TIME
10 MINUTES

COOK TIME
40 MINUTES

PER SERVING

CALORIES:
288

TOTAL FAT:
13 G

CARBS:
31 G

FIBER:
6 G

PROTEIN:
13 G

CALCIUM:
105 MG

VITAMIN D:
0 MCG

VITAMIN B12:
2 MCG

IRON:
3 MG

ZINC:
2 MG

Chickpea flour is a great gluten-free substitute for traditional flour. It forms the base of many veganized egg dishes and helps re-create breakfast dishes without soy. This frittata is a super-easy bistro-style brunch dish that pairs beautifully with lightly dressed mixed greens.

3 tablespoons extra-virgin olive oil, divided

1 large onion, diced

2 garlic cloves, minced

¾ cup fresh baby spinach leaves

2 tablespoons, plus 2¼ cups water, divided

1¾ cups chickpea flour

¼ cup nutritional yeast

½ teaspoon salt

1 teaspoon onion powder

½ teaspoon garlic powder

1 teaspoon baking powder

½ cup vegan Cheddar- or Parmesan-style shreds (optional)

1. Preheat the oven to 375°F and lightly grease a 9-inch pie dish with 1 tablespoon of olive oil.

2. In a medium skillet, heat the remaining 2 tablespoons of olive oil over medium-high heat. Add the onion and sauté until soft and golden but not browned. Add the garlic and cook for 1 minute.

3. Add the spinach and 2 tablespoons of water to the skillet. Cover with a lid and steam for 2 minutes. Remove the lid and continue to cook, stirring often, until the spinach is wilted. Set aside.

4. In a large bowl, combine the chickpea flour, nutritional yeast, salt, onion powder, garlic powder, and baking powder. Add the remaining 2¼ cups of water and whisk until combined.

5. Add the sautéed spinach, onion, and cheese, if using, to a large bowl. Stir to combine.

6. Pour the mix into the greased pie dish. Bake for 40 to 45 minutes or until a toothpick inserted in the center comes out clean. Let the dish cool for 10 minutes before slicing and serving.

VARIATION TIP: Turn these into on-the-go breakfast frittatas by baking them in a lightly greased muffin tin. Adjust the baking time to 30 to 35 minutes at 375°F.

Seedy Breakfast Cookies

These are my family's favorite cookies. My kids get excited when I make these because they know they'll get to eat them for breakfast. These cookies are filled with nuts, seeds, and fruit, making them healthy, protein packed, and sugar-free. I love the contrast between the sweet raisins and tart cranberries in these cookies, but you can change up the dried fruit to create your own signature flavor.

1 cup rolled oats	¼ cup chia seeds
¼ cup flaxseeds	3 tablespoons hemp hearts
2 overripe bananas	½ cup raisins
¼ cup unsweetened applesauce	¼ cup dried cranberries
2 tablespoons almond butter	¼ teaspoon ground cinnamon
½ cup slivered almonds	¼ teaspoon ground ginger
½ cup pumpkin seeds	¼ teaspoon ground nutmeg

1. Preheat the oven to 350°F. Line a large rimmed baking sheet with parchment.

2. Grind the rolled oats and flaxseeds in a blender or spice grinder.

3. In a large bowl, using a mixing spoon, mash together the bananas and applesauce. Add the almond butter, slivered almonds, oats, pumpkin seeds, flaxseeds, chia seeds, hemp hearts, raisins, cranberries, cinnamon, ginger, and nutmeg. Stir until the mixture forms a chunky batter.

4. Using a cookie or ice cream scoop, drop 1½-inch scoops of dough onto the prepared baking sheets. Flatten gently to form ½-inch thick rounds.

5. Bake for 17 to 20 minutes or until golden but not too dark. Let the cookies cool on the baking sheet for 5 minutes before transferring them to a wire rack to cool completely. Store in an airtight container for up to 5 days.

SUBSTITUTION TIP: To make these cookies nut-free, swap the almond butter for tahini or seed butter, and replace the slivered almonds with ½ cup of whole rolled oats. Use certified gluten-free oats to turn this recipe gluten-free.

MAKES
12 COOKIES

PREP TIME
5 MINUTES

COOK TIME
20 MINUTES

PER SERVING

CALORIES:
194

TOTAL FAT:
11 G

CARBS:
20 G

FIBER:
5 G

PROTEIN:
6 G

CALCIUM:
64 MG

VITAMIN D:
0 MCG

VITAMIN B12:
0 MCG

IRON:
2 MG

ZINC:
1 MG

Chickpea Western Omelet

SERVES
2 TO 3

PREP TIME
10 MINUTES

COOK TIME
10 MINUTES

PER SERVING

CALORIES:
391

TOTAL FAT:
24 G

CARBS:
28 G

FIBER:
8 G

PROTEIN:
19 G

CALCIUM:
68 MG

VITAMIN D:
0 MCG

VITAMIN B12:
21 MCG

IRON:
3 MG

ZINC:
1 MG

In my pre-vegan days, my favorite breakfast was a Western Omelet. In my humble opinion, all diners had to have a great Western Omelet. Omelets were one of the hardest things for me to give up when I became vegan. When I heard about chickpea omelets, I immediately went to work veganizing a Western Omelet. You can use this omelet base with any combination of fillings.

½ cup Smoky Tofu "Bacon" (page 18)
4 tablespoons extra-virgin olive oil, divided
½ medium onion, diced
½ green bell pepper, diced
1 cup chickpea flour

⅓ cup nutritional yeast
¼ teaspoon baking powder
½ teaspoon garlic powder
½ teaspoon onion powder
¼ teaspoon salt
¼ teaspoon pepper
1 cup water

1. Prepare Smoky Tofu "Bacon."

2. In a large nonstick skillet, heat 2 tablespoons of olive oil over medium-high heat. Add the onion and bell pepper and cook until soft, about 5 minutes. Add the tofu "bacon" and cook until warmed through. Transfer the vegetable and tofu mix to a medium bowl and set aside.

3. In a large bowl, combine the chickpea flour, nutritional yeast, baking powder, garlic powder, onion powder, salt, pepper, and water. Whisk into a batter.

4. Add the vegetable and tofu mixture to the batter and stir to incorporate.

5. Add the remaining 2 tablespoons of olive oil to the same skillet over medium-high heat. Pour ½ cup of batter into the pan and cook until the underside is browned, about 2 minutes. Flip and cook for 1 additional minute. Transfer to a plate. Repeat with the remaining batter and serve immediately.

VARIATION TIP: This recipe is very versatile. The omelet base is the same, but you can use a myriad of fillings. When in season, I love using fresh asparagus and mozzarella, or mushrooms and spinach.

Garlic and Dill Sunflower Seed Cream Cheese Bagels

MAKES
1½ CUPS
OF CREAM
CHEESE

PREP TIME
1 HOUR

Is there anything better than a bagel and shmear? It's a breakfast staple and is great for a quick on-the-go meal. This cream cheese also adds great flavor and richness to dishes like my Garlic Chive Red Mashed Potatoes (page 162). If you know you'll need to make this cream cheese quickly, soak the sunflower seeds ahead of time. When you're ready, you can whip everything up in just a few minutes!

PER SERVINGS

CALORIES:
636

TOTAL FAT:
37 G

CARBS:
58 G

FIBER:
13 G

PROTEIN:
25 G

CALCIUM:
174 MG

VITAMIN D:
0 MCG

VITAMIN B12:
1 MCG

IRON:
6 MG

ZINC:
5 MG

For the cream cheese

2 cups shelled sunflower seeds

3 cups hot water

2 tablespoons nutritional yeast

2 teaspoons apple cider vinegar

2 tablespoons lemon juice

1 teaspoon kosher salt

2 to 3 garlic cloves, minced

2 tablespoons chopped fresh dill

For the bagels

4 multigrain bagels, sliced in half

4 iceberg or butter lettuce leaves

½ red onion, thinly sliced

½ English cucumber, sliced into thin rounds

1 large tomato, sliced into thin rounds

3 tablespoon capers, drained

TO MAKE THE CREAM CHEESE

1. In a large bowl, combine the sunflower seeds and water and soak for 1 hour. Drain, rinse, and transfer the seeds to a food processor. Pulse until the sunflower seeds are crushed and resemble a paste.

2. Add the nutritional yeast, apple cider vinegar, lemon juice, salt, garlic, and dill to the food processor. Pulse until creamy, stopping to scrape down the sides as needed.

TO MAKE THE BAGELS

Spread the cream cheese on the bagels and top with lettuce, onion, cucumber, tomato, and capers. Serve immediately. Refrigerate extra cream cheese in an airtight container for up to 5 days.

Mixed Bean Salad

SERVES
4 TO 6

PREP TIME
15 MINUTES

This delicious and protein-packed salad will keep you energized all day. Its bright, fresh flavors remind me of summer on a dark and dreary winter day. If you're short on time, you can use a store-bought version of Catalina dressing—the Kraft version is inexpensive and vegan.

PER SERVING

CALORIES:
723

TOTAL FAT:
32 G

CARBS:
90 G

FIBER:
24 G

PROTEIN:
25 G

CALCIUM:
172 MG

VITAMIN D:
0 MCG

VITAMIN B12:
0 MCG

IRON:
7 MG

ZINC:
3 MG

For the Catalina dressing

¼ cup ketchup

¼ cup red wine vinegar

¼ cup granulated sugar

½ teaspoon onion powder

½ teaspoon paprika

¼ teaspoon soy sauce

½ cup vegetable oil

¼ teaspoon salt

¼ teaspoon ground black pepper

For the salad

1 (15-ounce) can lentils, drained and rinsed

1 (15-ounce) can kidney beans, drained and rinsed

1 (15-ounce) can white or navy beans, drained and rinsed

1 (15-ounce) can black beans, drained and rinsed

½ large red onion, diced

2 scallions, finely chopped

1 red bell pepper, diced

1 jalapeño, finely chopped (optional: remove white rib and seeds for less heat)

½ cup flat-leaf parsley, finely chopped

½ teaspoon salt

½ teaspoon ground black pepper

¾ cup Catalina dressing

TO MAKE THE CATALINA DRESSING

In a jar with a tight-fitting lid, combine the ketchup, red wine vinegar, sugar, onion powder, paprika, soy sauce, vegetable oil, salt, and black pepper. Shake well to combine.

TO MAKE THE SALAD

In a large bowl, combine the lentils, kidney beans, navy beans, black beans, red onion, scallions, bell pepper, jalapeño, parsley, salt, and pepper. Toss with the Catalina dressing and serve immediately. Refrigerate leftovers for up to 5 days.

STRETCH TIP: This salad gets better the longer it marinates, so I like to make a big batch on the weekend and store it in the fridge for a quick, healthy lunch all week long.

Curried Split Pea Soup

SERVES
4 TO 6

PREP TIME
10 MINUTES

COOK TIME
45 MINUTES

Split pea soup is a classic comfort food, especially in the winter when you're craving something warm and soothing. This hearty soup has a kick from a surprise ingredient—curry powder. It takes some time, but it's a "set it and forget it" recipe, meaning you don't have to watch over it on the stove for hours. I use yellow split peas for this recipe, but if you have green split peas on hand, they'll work just as well.

2 tablespoons extra-virgin olive oil

½ large onion, diced

1 to 2 tablespoons curry powder

½ teaspoon turmeric

1½ teaspoons salt

1 teaspoon ground black pepper

2 garlic cloves, minced

2 medium carrots, peeled and diced

3 red potatoes, skin on, cubed

6 cups vegetable broth

1 cup dried yellow (or green) split peas

PER SERVING

CALORIES:
233

TOTAL FAT:
5 G

CARBS:
42 G

FIBER:
8 G

PROTEIN:
7 G

CALCIUM:
53 MG

VITAMIN D:
0 MCG

VITAMIN B12:
0 MCG

IRON:
2 MG

ZINC:
1 MG

1. In a large soup pot, heat the oil over medium-high heat. Add the onion, curry powder, turmeric, salt, and pepper. Sauté until the onion is translucent and soft, about 5 minutes. Add the garlic and cook for 1 minute.

2. Add the carrots and potatoes to the pot and cook for one minute, stirring constantly. Pour in the vegetable broth and split peas. Stir to combine.

3. Bring to a boil, then reduce heat to medium-low and simmer, stirring occasionally, for 40 minutes, or until peas are soft.

4. Remove the soup from the heat and purée in small batches in a blender or use a hand blender to blend it in the pot, leaving it partially chunky to taste. Serve immediately and refrigerate leftovers.

VARIATION TIP: For a non-spicy version of this soup, swap the curry powder and turmeric for one teaspoon each of dried oregano and dill.

Chopped Chickpea Taco Salad

SERVES
4 TO 6

PREP TIME
20 MINUTES

PER SERVING

CALORIES:
709

TOTAL FAT:
30 G

CARBS:
93 G

FIBER:
23 G

PROTEIN:
23 G

CALCIUM:
234 MG

VITAMIN D:
2 MCG

VITAMIN B12:
1 MCG

IRON:
5 MG

ZINC:
3 MG

This salad is a huge crowd-pleaser at potluck dinners, and it's always one of the first dishes to get eaten. I like making it on the weekend and keeping it in the fridge for a ready-to-go protein-packed lunch or a light dinner. You can customize this salad to suit your tastes and what you have in the house—try using kidney beans, pinto beans, or even store-bought smoked tofu as your protein.

1 cup Vegan Caesar Dressing (page 33)
1 head iceberg lettuce, chopped
2 (15-ounce) cans chickpeas, drained and rinsed
1 (15-ounce) can black beans, drained and rinsed
2 plum tomatoes, seeded and diced
1 seedless cucumber, diced
1 (9-ounce) can corn
3 scallions, finely chopped
1 cup vegan Cheddar-style shreds
½ teaspoon dried dill
½ teaspoon dried parsley
1 teaspoon chili powder
½ cup salsa
1 cup crushed corn tortilla chips

1. Prepare the Vegan Caesar Dressing.

2. In a large bowl, combine the lettuce, chickpeas, black beans, tomatoes, cucumber, corn, scallions, and vegan Cheddar shreds.

3. In a small bowl, combine the Caesar dressing, dill, parsley, chili powder, and salsa. Stir to combine. Pour the mixture over the salad and toss well.

4. Top the salad with crushed tortilla chips. Serve immediately and refrigerate leftovers.

PREP TIP: If you plan on making this ahead of time, prep the salad, but leave the corn chips and dressing separate until serving time. This will keep your corn chips crispy and your lettuce from getting soggy.

Three-Bean Minestrone Soup

SERVES
4 TO 6

PREP TIME
10 MINUTES

COOK TIME
30 MINUTES

Minestrone soup is a great "clean out the fridge" recipe—aside from its tomato-sauce base, the ingredients can vary widely. Any vegetables you have lying around are fair game. I like to load mine up with different kinds of beans for extra protein. This soup is also a great way to use up any open boxes of pasta taking up space in your pantry.

PER SERVING

CALORIES:
394

TOTAL FAT:
8 G

CARBS:
64 G

FIBER:
19 G

PROTEIN:
21 G

CALCIUM:
254 MG

VITAMIN D:
0 MCG

VITAMIN B12:
2 MCG

IRON:
5 MG

ZINC:
2 MG

2 tablespoons extra-virgin olive oil
1 large onion, diced
1 large carrot, peeled and diced
2 celery stalks, diced
1 teaspoon dried oregano
1 teaspoon dried basil
2 garlic cloves, minced
6 cups vegetable broth
1 (28-ounce) can diced tomatoes, with liquid
1 (15-ounce) can crushed tomatoes

2 cups wax or green beans, sliced into ½-inch pieces
1 (15-ounce) can chickpeas, drained and rinsed
1 (15-ounce) can white beans, drained and rinsed
1 (15-ounce) can kidney beans, drained and rinsed
2 cups fresh baby spinach leaves
¼ cup nutritional yeast

1. In a large pot, heat the oil over medium-high heat. Add the onion and sauté until translucent, about 5 minutes. Add the carrot, celery, oregano, and basil, and cook until they begin to soften, about 5 minutes. Add the garlic and cook for 30 seconds.

2. Add the broth, diced tomatoes, and crushed tomatoes to the pot and stir to combine. Bring to a boil, then reduce heat and simmer uncovered for 10 minutes.

3. Add the wax or green beans, chickpeas, white beans, and kidney beans. Continue to simmer for 10 minutes or until all the vegetables are soft.

4. Remove from heat and toss in the spinach and nutritional yeast. Stir until the spinach wilts, about 2 minutes. Serve hot and refrigerate leftovers for up to a week.

Curried Chickpea Salad Wraps

I've been obsessed with this curried chickpea salad for years. I love its many different textures and bursts of flavor. The sweetness of mandarins and the tartness of dried cranberries balance the heat from the curry powder, and the Granny Smith apple adds great crunch. I serve this in a flour tortilla wrap, but you could make a gluten-free version by serving it in lettuce cups.

For the curried chickpea salad

3 tablespoons Easy 4-Ingredient Vegan Mayonnaise (page 21)

2 to 4 tablespoons mild curry powder, to taste

Juice of ½ lime

2 (15-ounce) cans chickpeas, drained and rinsed

1 Granny Smith apple, diced

1 (20-ounce) can mandarin orange segments, drained

½ cup dried cranberries

½ cup slivered or sliced almonds

For the wraps

4 flour tortillas

8 iceberg or butter lettuce leaves

TO MAKE THE CURRIED CHICKPEA SALAD

1. Prepare the Easy 4-Ingredient Vegan Mayonnaise. Then, in a small bowl, combine the mayonnaise, 2 tablespoons of curry powder, and lime juice.

2. In a large bowl, lightly mash the chickpeas, leaving some intact. Add the apple, mandarin oranges, cranberries, and almonds. Pour the curried mayonnaise into the bowl and stir to combine. Taste and add more curry powder if needed.

TO MAKE THE WRAPS

Layer each tortilla with lettuce and divide the chickpea mixture equally among them. Wrap the tortillas by pulling in the sides, then folding the bottom up, tucking in as you roll. Serve immediately and refrigerate leftovers.

VARIATION TIP: The chickpea salad is also delicious on crackers, as part of a charcuterie board, or served on toast at brunch. For a different texture and flavor, try swapping out the chickpeas for crumbled tempeh.

Lentil Soup

SERVES
4 TO 6

PREP TIME
5 MINUTES

COOK TIME
25 MINUTES

This is my go-to lentil soup recipe. It's hearty, rich, and full of bright flavor from the lemon zest and juice. The lentils break down nicely to give this soup a creamy consistency. To make it even creamier, stir in a little coconut milk or unsweetened soy creamer at the end. You could also serve it garnished with a swirl of cream and a drizzle of olive oil.

4 tablespoons extra-virgin olive
  oil, divided

1 large onion, diced

4 garlic cloves, minced

6 cups vegetable broth

1¼ cups dried red lentils, rinsed

½ cup white rice

1 tablespoon cumin

½ teaspoon salt

½ teaspoon ground black pepper

1 teaspoon lemon zest

Juice of 1 lemon

1. In a large pot, heat 3 tablespoons of olive oil over medium-high heat. Add the onion and cook for 3 to 5 minutes, until soft but not browned. Add the garlic and cook for 30 seconds.

2. Pour in the vegetable broth and bring it to a boil. Add the lentils, rice, cumin, salt, pepper, and lemon zest. Stir to combine. Cook at a rolling boil for 20 minutes, or until the lentils are soft.

3. Remove from the heat. Stir in the remaining tablespoon of olive oil and the lemon juice. Adjust salt and pepper to taste. Serve immediately and refrigerate leftovers.

VARIATION TIP: Add some carrots to this soup. Peel and slice 2 carrots and let them cook with the rice and lentils. After 20 minutes, they'll be a soft, delicious addition to the soup. You could also chop up some kale and toss it into the soup to wilt for the last 5 minutes of cooking.

PER SERVING

CALORIES:
281

TOTAL FAT:
10 G

CARBS:
37 G

FIBER:
3 G

PROTEIN:
13 G

CALCIUM:
42 MG

VITAMIN D:
0 MCG

VITAMIN B12:
0 MCG

IRON:
1 MG

ZINC:
0 MG

White Bean Chili

This easy dish is a nice change from the more common tomato-based, dark vegetable chili. This recipe uses cumin, oregano, and green chilis that complement the flavors and heat of a typical chili. The light-colored beans give this dish a striking appearance, and they're also a great source of protein. The best part about this chili: It relies on ingredients you likely already have on hand and comes together in about half an hour, making it a perfect weeknight dinner.

SERVES
4 TO 6

PREP TIME
10 MINUTES

COOK TIME
25 MINUTES

PER SERVING

CALORIES:
340

TOTAL FAT:
10 G

CARBS:
50 G

FIBER:
17 G

PROTEIN:
16 G

CALCIUM:
163 MG

VITAMIN D:
0 MCG

VITAMIN B12:
0 MCG

IRON:
4 MG

ZINC:
1 MG

3 tablespoons extra-virgin olive oil
1 medium onion, diced
2 celery stalks, diced
1 carrot, diced
2 garlic cloves, minced
1 teaspoon dried oregano
2 teaspoons ground cumin
½ teaspoon salt
½ teaspoon ground black pepper
1 (4-ounce) can green chilis (or one jalapeño, seeded and diced)
1 (15-ounce) can white kidney beans, drained and rinsed
1 (15-ounce) can chickpeas, drained and rinsed
1 (15-ounce) can navy beans, drained and rinsed
2 cups vegetable broth
2 cups kale, chopped or shredded

1. Heat the olive oil in a large pot over medium-high heat. Add the onion, celery, and carrot. Cook for 8 to 10 minutes, until the vegetables soften. Add the garlic, oregano, cumin, salt, pepper, and green chilis. Cook for 2 minutes.

2. Add the kidney beans, chickpeas, navy beans, broth, and kale. Bring to a rolling boil and cook for 6 to 8 minutes or until the kale is soft. Remove from heat and serve hot.

VARIATION TIP: To take this chili to the next level, serve it with a spread of toppings and garnishes, like vegan sour cream, vegan Cheddar-style shreds, chopped avocado, sliced jalapeños, and corn tortilla chips on the side for some crunch.

Chickpea Cauliflower Burgers

SERVES
4

PREP TIME
5 MINUTES

COOK TIME
30 MINUTES

This is a fun variation on a veggie burger that packs a lot of whole-food protein into a single patty. I like to serve it fully loaded on a bun with avocado, Quick Caramelized Onions (page 19), and Lemon Tahini Vinaigrette (page 34), but it's also great with some lightly dressed mixed greens. This recipe uses bread crumbs as a binder, but you could make it gluten-free by using gluten-free bread crumbs or one cup of leftover cooked rice instead.

PER SERVING

CALORIES:
817

TOTAL FAT:
35 G

CARBS:
103 G

FIBER:
25 G

PROTEIN:
31 G

CALCIUM:
235 MG

VITAMIN D:
0 MCG

VITAMIN B12:
0 MCG

IRON:
8 MG

ZINC:
4 MG

For the patties

1 head cauliflower, chopped into florets
5 tablespoons extra-virgin olive oil, divided
½ teaspoon salt
1 (15-ounce) can chickpeas, drained and rinsed
1 (15-ounce) can red lentils, drained and rinsed
½ cup chopped flat-leaf parsley
½ teaspoon sriracha or other hot sauce
zest of 1 lemon
1 teaspoon paprika
½ teaspoon cumin
½ teaspoon garlic powder
½ teaspoon onion powder
½ teaspoon ground black pepper
1 cup bread crumbs

For serving

1 tablespoon Lemon Tahini Vinaigrette (page 34)
½ cup Quick Caramelized Onions (page 19)
4 burger buns
8 iceberg or butter lettuce leaves
1 large tomato, thinly sliced
1 avocado, pitted and sliced

TO MAKE THE PATTIES

1. Preheat the oven to 425°F.

2. Line a large rimmed baking sheet with parchment paper. Spread the cauliflower florets onto the baking sheet and toss with 2 tablespoons of olive oil and salt. Roast for 20 minutes. Set aside to cool.

CONTINUED >

Chickpea Cauliflower Burgers, CONTINUED

3. Add the cooled cauliflower to a food processor with the chickpeas, lentils, parsley, sriracha, lemon zest, paprika, cumin, garlic powder, onion powder, black pepper, and bread crumbs. Process until the mixture sticks. Remove from the food processor and divide into patties.

4. Using a wide frying pan, heat the remaining 3 tablespoons of olive oil and add the cauliflower patties to the pan. Cook for about 5 minutes, or until the bottom is golden. Flip and cook the other side for 2 to 3 minutes.

TO SERVE

1. While the cauliflower roasts, prepare the Lemon Tahini Vinaigrette and Quick Caramelized Onions.

2. Place the patties on the buns with lettuce, tomato, avocado, caramelized onions, and dressing.

TECHNIQUE TIP: If you're not a fan of panfrying, try baking these burgers in the oven instead. Heat the oven to 400°F and place the patties on a large parchment-lined baking sheet. Bake for 30 minutes, flipping the patties halfway through.

Lentil and Mushroom Sweet Potato Shepherd's Pie

SERVES
4 TO 6

PREP TIME
10 MINUTES

COOK TIME
35 MINUTES

Shepherd's pie is one of those dishes that feels like it should take hours to make. You really can spend hours making it, but since I'm often pressed for time, I like this "cheat" version. I've swapped the traditional mashed potato topping for sweet potatoes, which are healthier and can be cooked in the microwave while you're prepping the filling. Canned lentils and frozen vegetables are great time savers here, allowing you to get this dinner on the table in under 45 minutes.

5 large sweet potatoes

2 tablespoons extra-virgin olive oil

1 medium onion, diced

3 garlic cloves, minced

8 ounces cremini mushrooms, thinly sliced

1 (15-ounce) can lentils, drained and rinsed

1 tablespoon tomato paste

2 tablespoons soy sauce

1 teaspoon dried oregano

1 teaspoon dried basil

½ teaspoon dried thyme

2 cups vegetable broth

2 cups frozen peas and carrots

2 tablespoons all-purpose flour

¼ cup vegan butter

½ cup unsweetened soy milk

½ teaspoon salt

¼ teaspoon ground cinnamon

¼ teaspoon ground black pepper

PER SERVING

CALORIES:
402

TOTAL FAT:
13 G

CARBS:
61 G

FIBER:
12 G

PROTEIN:
14 G

CALCIUM:
130 MG

VITAMIN D:
11 MCG

VITAMIN B12:
0 MCG

IRON:
5 MG

ZINC:
2 MG

1. Preheat the oven to 400°F. Grease a 9-by-11-inch baking dish.

2. Prep the sweet potatoes for the microwave by poking holes all over each sweet potato with a fork or knife. Microwave them for 12 to 15 minutes, or until a knife slides through the center of each potato easily. Remove the potatoes from the microwave, cut each open lengthwise, and set aside to cool.

3. While the sweet potatoes are in the microwave, make the filling. Heat the olive oil in a deep pan over medium-high heat. Add the onion and cook until soft, about 5 minutes. Add the garlic, mushrooms, and lentils. Cook for 7 to 10 minutes, stirring frequently, until the mushrooms are soft.

CONTINUED >

Lentil and Mushroom Sweet Potato Shepherd's Pie, CONTINUED

4. Add the tomato paste, soy sauce, oregano, basil, thyme, and vegetable broth. Stir to combine. Reduce the heat and simmer for 10 minutes. Add the peas and carrots and stir until warmed through.

5. Add the flour and stir until the mixture thickens. Remove from heat and set aside.

6. Peel the sweet potatoes. In a large bowl, combine the sweet potatoes, butter, milk, salt, cinnamon, and pepper. Use a potato masher or fork to mash together.

7. Scoop the mushroom and lentil filling into the greased baking dish and spread in an even layer. Top with the mashed sweet potatoes. Bake for 10 minutes or until the sweet potatoes are golden. Serve warm.

VARIATION TIP: Take this recipe to another level by serving it with a drizzle of Mushroom Gravy (page 35) on top. If you're not a fan of lentils, you could swap them out for chickpeas or simply double up on mushrooms instead.

Chana Masala

SERVES
4

PREP TIME
10 MINUTES

COOK TIME
15 MINUTES

PER SERVING

CALORIES:
388

TOTAL FAT:
19 G

CARBS:
43 G

FIBER:
10 G

PROTEIN:
11 G

CALCIUM:
130 MG

VITAMIN D:
0 MCG

VITAMIN B12:
0 MCG

IRON:
3 MG

ZINC:
1 MG

Chana masala is an Indian dish made with chickpeas, onions, and tomatoes in a rich, warm curry sauce. It's wonderful served over basmati rice or with naan. I've even served it over Garlic Chive Red Mashed Potatoes (page 162) when I needed to use up leftovers. You can adjust the heat of this curry by adding more or less curry paste while cooking or by adding some diced chilis into the dish.

2 to 3 tablespoons Basic Curry
   Paste (page 20)
2 tablespoons extra-virgin olive oil
1 large onion, diced
2 garlic cloves, minced
2 (15-ounce) cans chickpeas,
   drained and rinsed
1 (28-ounce) can diced tomatoes,
   strained

1 cup vegetable broth
1 cup canned coconut milk
2 tablespoons cornstarch
¼ cup cold water
¼ cup fresh flat-leaf parsley or
   cilantro, chopped for garnish
   (optional)

1. Prepare the Basic Curry Paste.

2. In a deep pan or Dutch oven, heat the oil over medium-high heat. Add the onion and cook until soft and translucent, about 5 minutes. Add the garlic and curry paste and cook until fragrant, about 1 minute.

3. Add the chickpeas, tomatoes, vegetable broth, and coconut milk. Stir to combine and simmer for 10 minutes.

4. In a small bowl, make a cornstarch slurry by mixing the cornstarch in the water, stirring until no lumps remain.

5. Add the cornstarch slurry to the chickpeas. Cook for 3 to 5 minutes, stirring frequently, until the sauce thickens enough to coat the back of a spoon. Remove the chana masala from the heat, garnish with the parsley, if using, and serve on its own or over your favorite grain.

VARIATION TIP: Although chana masala typically uses only chickpeas, you can change up this dish by adding other vegetables to it, like diced potatoes, cauliflower, green beans, okra, spinach, or squash. Go through your fridge or freezer and use what you've got.

Lentil Meatballs with Mushroom Gravy

SERVES
4

PREP TIME
10 MINUTES

COOK TIME
20 MINUTES

PER SERVING

CALORIES:
455

TOTAL FAT:
20 G

CARBS:
54 G

FIBER:
12 G

PROTEIN:
19 G

CALCIUM:
85 MG

VITAMIN D:
2 MCG

VITAMIN B12:
2 MCG

IRON:
6 MG

ZINC:
3 MG

I love making this dish on a cold, wintery night. I live in a climate where winter is real . . . and cold. There are plenty of opportunities for comfort food dishes like this one. The meatballs are full of flavor and pair well with Mushroom Gravy (page 35) and a mountain of Garlic Chive Red Mashed Potatoes (page 162). I use lentils for this recipe, but it works just as well with black beans.

2 cups Mushroom Gravy (page 35)
1 tablespoon ground flaxseed
3 tablespoons hot water
2 tablespoons extra-virgin olive oil
1 medium onion, diced
2 garlic cloves, minced
1 (15-ounce) can lentils, drained and rinsed
1 tablespoon tomato paste

1 teaspoon soy sauce
1 teaspoon dried oregano
1 teaspoon dried basil
½ teaspoon dried thyme
¼ teaspoon red pepper flakes
¼ cup nutritional yeast
½ cup bread crumbs
½ teaspoon salt
½ teaspoon ground black pepper

1. Preheat the oven to 375°F. Line a large rimmed baking sheet with parchment paper and set aside.

2. Prepare the Mushroom Gravy.

3. Make a flaxseed egg by combining 1 tablespoon of ground flaxseed with 3 tablespoons of hot water. Stir and let sit until thick, about 5 minutes.

4. In a skillet, heat the extra-virgin olive oil over medium-high heat. Add the onion and cook for 5 to 7 minutes, until soft and golden. Add the garlic and cook for one minute, stirring constantly to prevent burning.

5. Transfer the onions and garlic to a bowl or food processor and add the flaxseed egg, lentils, tomato paste, soy sauce, oregano, basil, thyme, red pepper flakes, nutritional yeast, bread crumbs, salt, and pepper. Mix well or pulse until the ingredients form a dough.

6. If using a food processor, remove the blade. Scoop the dough into a bowl. Using a large spoon or ice cream scoop, scoop the dough and roll gently into 1-inch balls. Place the balls on the prepared baking sheet and bake for 10 to 15 minutes.

7. While the meatballs cook, warm the gravy over medium-high heat until just bubbling, 5 to 10 minutes.

8. Remove the meatballs from the oven and let sit for 5 minutes to set. Serve with the Mushroom Gravy.

VARIATION TIP: Want to switch up spaghetti night? These meatballs are fabulous with spaghetti, marinara sauce, and a bit of nutritional yeast or vegan parmesan sprinkled on top. Try frying the meatballs in a frying pan with a bit of oil first to get them crispy on the outside, then finish them off in the oven at 375°F for 15 to 20 minutes.

Chickpea Stew with Dumplings

SERVES
4

PREP TIME
15 MINUTES

COOK TIME
30 MINUTES

PER SERVING

CALORIES:
541

TOTAL FAT:
15 G

CARBS:
87 G

FIBER:
17 G

PROTEIN:
19 G

CALCIUM:
300 MG

VITAMIN D:
15 MCG

VITAMIN B12:
0 MCG

IRON:
5 MG

ZINC:
1 MG

This vegan take on a classic chicken-and-dumplings recipe features fluffy dumplings in a hearty, rich stew that's loaded with chickpeas, potatoes and carrots. I like to add leeks to this dish for their mild, bright flavor. Try changing up the ingredients in the dumpling batter—add chives, vegan Cheddar shreds, ground black pepper, or diced jalapeños. The possibilities are endless.

3 tablespoons extra-virgin olive oil

1 medium onion, diced

1 leek, washed, halved, and thinly sliced into half moons (white part only)

2 garlic cloves, minced

2 to 3 medium yellow potatoes, diced

2 large carrots, peeled and diced

1 large sweet potato, peeled and diced

1 teaspoon dried oregano

1 teaspoon dried basil

1 cup all-purpose flour, divided

1¾ teaspoons baking powder

½ teaspoon salt

½ teaspoon dried dill

½ teaspoon dried parsley

½ cup, plus 2 tablespoons unsweetened soy milk

3 cups vegetable broth, divided

1½ vegan chicken bouillon cubes

1 (15-ounce) can chickpeas, drained and rinsed

1 cup fresh or frozen peas

½ teaspoon ground black pepper

1. In a stock pot, heat the olive oil over medium-high heat. Add the onions, leeks, garlic, potatoes, carrots, sweet potato, oregano, and basil. Cook for 8 to 10 minutes, until the onions and leeks are soft and translucent.

2. While the onions and leeks cook, make the dumpling batter. In a small bowl, combine ¾ cup flour, the baking powder, salt, dill, parsley and ½ cup milk. Whisk to combine. If the batter is too thick to pour, add additional milk, 1 tablespoon at a time, to thin it.

3. Add the remaining ¼ cup of flour to the pot of vegetables and stir to coat. Add ½ cup vegetable broth and cook until the broth evaporates and the flour is cooked through.

4. Add the bouillon cubes and the remaining 2½ cups broth, along with the chickpeas, peas, and pepper. Stir to incorporate. Bring the soup to a boil and reduce the heat to low.

5. Drop heaping tablespoons of the dumpling batter into the pot, spaced apart. Cover and simmer on low for 20 minutes, or until the potatoes are tender and the dumplings are firm to the touch. Serve immediately.

TECHNIQUE TIP: To prepare a leek, remove the bulb and the dark green tops and slice the remaining root down the middle. Run the leek under cold water to remove any sand that might be stuck in each layer, and then slice them into half-moon shapes.

Curried Kidney Bean Burritos

SERVES
4 TO 6

PREP TIME
10 MINUTES

COOK TIME
25 MINUTES

PER SERVING

CALORIES:
398

TOTAL FAT:
16 G

CARBS:
55 G

FIBER:
14 G

PROTEIN:
14 G

CALCIUM:
175 MG

VITAMIN D:
0 MCG

VITAMIN B12:
0 MCG

IRON:
4 MG

ZINC:
1 MG

This dish is an ode to my love of Indian and Mexican cuisines. The burrito filling is inspired by an Indian dish called *rajma*, made of kidney beans cooked in a spiced tomato-based curry. The traditional dish doesn't contain carrots or potatoes, but I had some to use up one day, so I added them in. I like to eat this filling in burritos, but it's excellent over rice as well.

For the filling

2 tablespoons Basic Curry Paste (page 20)

3 tablespoons extra-virgin olive oil

1 medium onion, diced

1 large yellow potato, diced small

1 carrot, peeled and diced small

2 garlic cloves, minced

1 cup tomato sauce

1 (15-ounce) can red kidney beans, drained and rinsed

1 (15-ounce) can white kidney beans, drained and rinsed

1 jalapeño, diced

1 cup water

For the burritos

½ head iceberg lettuce, chopped or shredded

6 large flour tortillas

1 cup vegan sour cream

TO MAKE THE FILLING

1. Prepare the Basic Curry Paste.

2. In a large pan, heat the oil over medium-high heat. Add the onion, potato, and carrot. Cook for 8 to 10 minutes, until the onion is translucent and the potato and carrot are soft.

3. Add the garlic and curry paste and cook for 1 to 2 minutes or until fragrant.

4. Add the tomato sauce, red and white kidney beans, jalapeño, and water. Bring to a boil, then reduce heat to medium and simmer, uncovered, for 10 minutes or until chunky. Remove from the heat.

TO MAKE THE BURRITOS

1. Place the shredded lettuce down the middle of each tortilla. Using a slotted spoon, add about 3 tablespoons of the kidney bean stew on top of each pile of lettuce. Top with a dollop of vegan sour cream. Roll the burrito by folding in the sides, then rolling the bottom up, tucking it under as you roll toward the top. Repeat with the remaining tortillas.

2. Drizzle each burrito with the remaining kidney bean stew and another dollop of sour cream. Serve immediately.

STRETCH TIP: Do you have leftover rice in your fridge? Add it to your burritos in place of lettuce and turn these into a great freezer/make-ahead meal. Follow the recipe, stopping after step 3. Store the burritos and leftover kidney bean mix in freezer-safe containers until ready to serve.

Butternut Squash and Mixed Bean Soup

SERVES
4 TO 6

PREP TIME
10 MINUTES

COOK TIME
25 MINUTES

PER SERVING

CALORIES:
441

TOTAL FAT:
13 G

CARBS:
62 G

FIBER:
17 G

PROTEIN:
19 G

CALCIUM:
136 MG

VITAMIN D:
0 MCG

VITAMIN B12:
0 MCG

IRON:
4 MG

ZINC:
2 MG

This soup was inspired by another butternut squash soup I've made for years that needed refreshing. Most butternut squash soups I've tasted are puréed, but I wanted one with more texture and protein—hence all the beans. I love this soup because the coconut milk makes the broth smooth and creamy, but the soup is still chunky and hearty.

2 tablespoons extra-virgin olive oil
1 medium onion, diced
1 red bell pepper, diced
1 large yellow potato, diced small
1 (15-ounce) can chickpeas, drained and rinsed
1 (15-ounce) can kidney beans, drained and rinsed
1 (15-ounce) can navy beans, drained and rinsed

2 cups frozen, diced, butternut squash
½ teaspoon dried thyme
½ teaspoon cumin
½ teaspoon paprika
¼ teaspoon smoked paprika
1½ cups vegetable broth
1 cup canned coconut milk

1. In a deep pot, heat the oil over medium-high heat. Add the onion, bell pepper, and potato. Sauté for about 4 minutes, until the onions are soft and translucent and just starting to look golden but not browned.

2. Add the chickpeas, kidney beans, navy beans, butternut squash, thyme, cumin, paprika, and smoked paprika. Stir to coat.

3. Pour in the vegetable broth and coconut milk. Bring to a boil, then reduce heat to medium. Simmer for 15 to 20 minutes before serving. Refrigerate leftovers.

VARIATION TIP: Try adding green beans, spinach, or kale to this dish for a boost of flavor and color. To turn it into a stew, reduce the amount of vegetable broth by ½ cup and serve over rice.

Hearty Vegetarian Chili

SERVES
4 TO 6

PREP TIME
10 MINUTES

COOK TIME
30 MINUTES

This is my go-to chili recipe, and it's always a hit at parties and pot-lucks. It's also very customizable. To mix it up, try adding bell peppers, corn, black beans, or cubed sweet potatoes. You can also dial up the heat by adding more jalapeño or a hot sauce like sriracha.

2 tablespoons extra-virgin olive oil

1 large onion, diced

6 ounces cremini mushrooms, thinly sliced

2 stalks celery, diced

2 carrots, peeled and diced

1 jalapeño, finely chopped

2 cloves garlic, minced

1 zucchini, diced

1 (15-ounce) can diced tomatoes, drained

1 (15-ounce) can kidney beans, drained and rinsed

1 (15-ounce) can black beans, drained and rinsed

1 (15-ounce) can pinto beans, drained and rinsed

3 cups tomato sauce

1 cup water

2 tablespoons chili powder

1 tablespoon brown sugar

½ teaspoon smoked paprika

1 tablespoon soy sauce

2 tablespoons ketchup

1 teaspoon yellow mustard

Vegan sour cream, for garnish (optional)

Vegan Cheddar-style shreds, for garnish (optional)

1 scallion, finely chopped, for garnish (optional)

1. In a deep pot or Dutch oven, heat the oil over medium-high heat. Add the onion, mushrooms, celery, and carrots. Cook until the onion is translucent and vegetables soften, about 5 minutes. Add the jalapeño, garlic, zucchini, and diced tomatoes. Stir and cook for 2 minutes.

2. Add the kidney beans, black beans, pinto beans, tomato sauce, and water to the pot. Stir to combine.

3. Add the chili powder, brown sugar, smoked paprika, soy sauce, ketchup, and mustard. Stir well. Bring to a boil, then reduce heat to medium and simmer for 20 minutes before serving.

4. Optional: Top the chili with sour cream, vegan Cheddar-style shreds, and scallion.

VARIATION TIP: Mix this chili with leftover cooked rice and use it as a filling for burritos, enchiladas, or stuffed peppers; or on top of nachos.

PER SERVING

CALORIES:
409

TOTAL FAT:
7 G

CARBS:
70 G

FIBER:
21 G

PROTEIN:
21 G

CALCIUM:
217 MG

VITAMIN D:
1 MCG

VITAMIN B12:
0 MCG

IRON:
6 MG

ZINC:
3 MG

Black Bean Burgers

SERVES
4

PREP TIME
20 MINUTES

COOK TIME
20 MINUTES

PER SERVING

CALORIES:
736

TOTAL FAT:
24 G

CARBS:
109 G

FIBER:
22 G

PROTEIN:
28 G

CALCIUM:
428 MG

VITAMIN D:
2 MCG

VITAMIN B12:
0 MCG

IRON:
7 MG

ZINC:
4 MG

I love a well-seasoned burger—one that tastes good even if it is eaten without a bun or toppings. I've tested dozens of vegan burger recipes trying to find the right balance of seasoning and meatiness, and this one is by far my favorite. The caramelized mushrooms and onions give this burger an amazing flavor, and the combination of beans and rice give it a great texture, just like the kind you'd expect from your local diner.

For the patties

4 tablespoons extra-virgin olive oil, divided

1 large onion, chopped

4 ounces cremini mushrooms, thinly sliced (about 1¼ cups)

1 cup cooked rice

1 cup panko bread crumbs

1 (15-ounce) can black beans, drained and rinsed

2 garlic cloves, minced

1 tablespoon soy sauce

2 tablespoons ketchup

1 teaspoon salt

½ teaspoon ground black pepper

1 tablespoon chili powder

1 teaspoon cumin

1 teaspoon onion powder

1 teaspoon nutritional yeast

For the burgers

4 black bean patties

4 hamburger buns

4 iceberg or butter lettuce leaves

½ large tomato, thinly sliced

4 vegan cheese slices

½ onion, thinly sliced

Ketchup

Mustard

TO MAKE THE PATTIES

1. In a deep skillet, heat 2 tablespoons of oil over medium-high heat. Add the onion and mushrooms. Sauté for 7 to 8 minutes, until both are soft and golden. Remove the onion and mushroom mixture and put them in a food processor.

2. In the food processor, add the rice, panko bread crumbs, black beans, garlic, soy sauce, ketchup, salt, pepper, chili powder, cumin, onion powder, and nutritional yeast. Pulse until a chunky mixture forms.

3. Divide the mixture and shape into four equal patties, and refrigerate for 15 minutes.

4. In a deep skillet, heat the remaining 2 tablespoons of olive oil over medium-high heat. Add the patties, spacing them apart evenly. Cook for 4 to 5 minutes on one side, flip, and cook for 3 to 4 minutes.

TO MAKE THE BURGERS

Assemble the burgers on buns and garnish with lettuce, tomato, cheese, and onion and 1 tablespoon each ketchup and mustard per burger.

TECHNIQUE TIP: These burgers can also be baked without oil in the oven. Line a large rimmed baking sheet with parchment paper and bake at 375°F for 25 minutes, flipping halfway through.

BBQ Pulled Jackfruit Sandwiches, 109

5

Fruits, Vegetables, Mushrooms, and More

Peanut Butter Banana Flaxseed French Toast

SERVES
4

PREP TIME
5 MINUTES

COOK TIME
20 MINUTES

PER SERVING

CALORIES:
867

TOTAL FAT:
58 G

CARBS:
71 G

FIBER:
14 G

PROTEIN:
16 G

CALCIUM:
368 MG

VITAMIN D:
50 MCG

VITAMIN B12:
0 MCG

IRON:
4 MG

ZINC:
0 MG

My brother was a huge French toast fan growing up, so I created this veganized version for him. I use peanut butter and banana in this recipe, but you can easily switch it up with different fruit and spread combinations, like sliced strawberries or peaches with jam. To make this dish extra decadent, stuff the French toast with chocolate chips and top it with powdered sugar (and more chocolate chips, of course)!

1 tablespoon ground flaxseed
3 tablespoons hot water
2 cups almond milk
1½ tablespoons ground cinnamon
½ tablespoon ground nutmeg
2 tablespoons granulated sugar

8 tablespoons vegan
  butter, divided
8 slices whole grain bread
1 cup smooth peanut butter
3 ripe bananas, sliced

1. Make a flaxseed egg by combining 1 tablespoon of ground flaxseed with 3 tablespoons of hot water. Stir and let it sit for 5 minutes until thickened.

2. In a shallow dish, combine the flaxseed egg, almond milk, cinnamon, nutmeg, and sugar. Set aside.

3. Melt 2 tablespoons of vegan butter in a nonstick skillet over medium heat.

4. Dip two slices of bread in the almond milk dish for 3 to 5 seconds each. Remove and let the excess milk drip back into the bowl.

5. Spread 4 tablespoon of peanut butter on one slice of bread and top with 4 to 5 banana slices. Finish the sandwich with the other slice of bread.

6. Place the sandwich in the skillet with the melted butter and cook for 3 to 4 minutes per side. Transfer to a plate. Repeat with remaining bread slices. Serve immediately.

SUBSTITUTION TIP: You can easily make this dish nut-free by swapping the peanut butter for roasted soy butter or any other seed butter.

Blueberry Pancakes

SERVES
2 TO 3

PREP TIME
10 MINUTES

COOK TIME
15 MINUTES

With this simple recipe, it's easy to make fluffy, soft, diner-style pancakes in your own kitchen. The trick for achieving that signature diner-pancake taste is buttermilk, a fermented milk made by adding an acid to milk and letting it curdle. For this recipe, I've added fresh lemon juice to unsweetened soy milk to achieve that same tangy flavor.

1 tablespoon ground flaxseed

3 tablespoons hot water

1 cup unsweetened soy milk

1 tablespoon lemon juice

1 cup all-purpose flour

1 tablespoon granulated sugar

1 tablespoon baking powder

½ teaspoon salt

½ teaspoon grated lemon zest

2 tablespoons vegetable oil

1 teaspoon vanilla extract

2 cups fresh blueberries, divided

2 to 3 tablespoons powdered sugar, for dusting (optional)

1. Make a flaxseed egg by combining the ground flaxseed with the hot water. Stir and let it sit for 5 minutes until thickened.

2. In a measuring glass, combine the soy milk with the lemon juice and let it stand for 5 minutes to curdle into vegan buttermilk.

3. In a large bowl, sift together the flour, sugar, baking powder, and salt.

4. Add the lemon zest, buttermilk, vegetable oil, and vanilla extract. Whisk to form a batter. Gently fold in 1 cup of blueberries.

5. Heat a large nonstick pan over medium heat. When the pan is hot, add one ladle of pancake batter to the pan. Cook for 3 to 4 minutes, until the bottom is browned. Flip the pancake over and cook for 1 to 2 minutes. Transfer to a plate. Repeat with the remaining batter.

6. Top the pancakes with the remaining 1 cup of blueberries and dust with powdered sugar, if using. Serve immediately.

VARIATION TIP: I love blueberries, but you can make these pancakes using whatever fruit is in season. Try swapping the blueberries for fresh raspberries or strawberries in summer months. In the winter, when fresh berries are more expensive or harder to come by, try using bananas instead.

PER SERVING

CALORIES:
347

TOTAL FAT:
12 G

CARBS:
52 G

FIBER:
8 G

PROTEIN:
10 G

CALCIUM:
300 MG

VITAMIN D:
0 MCG

VITAMIN B12:
0 MCG

IRON:
3 MG

ZINC:
0 MG

Cinnamon Orange French Toast with Quick Raspberry Coulis

SERVES
4

PREP TIME
10 MINUTES

COOK TIME
20 MINUTES

PER SERVING

CALORIES:
583

TOTAL FAT:
26 G

CARBS:
84 G

FIBER:
13 G

PROTEIN:
6 G

CALCIUM:
335 MG

VITAMIN D:
50 MCG

VITAMIN B12:
0 MCG

IRON:
3 MG

ZINC:
0 MG

This restaurant-style French toast looks like it takes forever to make, but it actually comes together in about 30 minutes. The combination of cinnamon, sugar, orange, and raspberries reminds me of the holidays, so I often make this for Christmas breakfast. For the coulis, try using different berries, like blueberries, blackberries, and strawberries—they all pair well with orange and cinnamon.

For the raspberry coulis

½ cup granulated sugar

3 tablespoons orange juice

1½ cups fresh raspberries

For the French toast

1 tablespoon ground flaxseed

3 tablespoons hot water

2 cups almond milk

1½ tablespoons ground cinnamon

½ tablespoon ground nutmeg

2 tablespoons granulated sugar

3 tablespoons orange zest

2 tablespoons orange juice

8 tablespoons vegan butter

8 slices of whole grain bread

¼ cup powdered sugar, for dusting (optional)

½ cup raspberries

TO MAKE THE RASPBERRY COULIS

1. In a medium saucepan, combine the sugar, orange juice and raspberries. Gently cook for 4 to 6 minutes over medium heat until the sugar dissolves and the raspberries break down.

2. Remove the raspberry mixture from the heat and strain through a mesh sieve to remove seeds. Set aside.

TO MAKE THE FRENCH TOAST

1. Make a flaxseed egg by combining the ground flaxseed with the hot water. Stir and let it sit for 5 minutes until thickened.

2. In a shallow dish, combine the flaxseed egg, almond milk, cinnamon, nutmeg, sugar, orange zest, and orange juice. Set aside.

3. Melt 2 tablespoons of vegan butter in a large nonstick pan over medium heat.

4. Dip two slices of bread into the almond milk for 3 to 5 seconds. Remove and let the excess milk drip back into the bowl.

5. Place the dipped bread in the pan and cook for 3 to 4 minutes per side. Transfer to a plate. Dust with the powdered sugar, if using, and drizzle with the raspberry coulis and the remaining fresh raspberries. Repeat with the remaining bread slices.

TECHNIQUE TIP: If you don't have fresh raspberries for your sauce, use frozen. Thaw them ahead of time by refrigerating 2 cups of frozen raspberries overnight. Alternatively, heat them in a saucepan for 2 to 3 minutes before adding the orange juice and sugar.

Fresh Fruit Crepes with Dark Chocolate Sauce

Crepes are fun and easy to make. I love serving them for brunch and giving my guests a variety of different fillings, such as fresh fruits, chocolate spreads, peanut butter, powdered sugar, whipped coconut cream, and Quick Raspberry Coulis (page 94). To prepare these for a crowd, transfer the cooked crepes to an oven-safe dish and keep them warm in the oven at 200°F.

For the chocolate sauce

½ cup almond milk (sweetened or unsweetened)

1 teaspoon vanilla extract

½ cup maple syrup

¼ cup coconut oil, melted

½ cup Dutch-processed cocoa powder

For the crepes

1½ cups all-purpose flour

3 tablespoons granulated sugar

1 teaspoon baking powder

2 tablespoons extra-virgin olive oil

1½ to 2 cups soy milk, divided

2 large bananas, sliced

2 cups sliced fresh strawberries

¼ cup powdered sugar, for dusting (optional)

TO MAKE THE CHOCOLATE SAUCE

1. In a small saucepan over medium-low heat, combine the almond milk, vanilla extract, the maple syrup, and coconut oil. Bring to a low simmer.

2. Add the cocoa powder and whisk to combine. Simmer for 3 minutes, uncovered. Set aside.

TO MAKE THE CREPES

1. In a large bowl, combine the flour, sugar, baking powder, olive oil, and 1½ cups of soy milk. Whisk to form a batter slightly thinner than pancake batter. If the mix is too thick, add the remaining ½ cup of soy milk, a tablespoon at a time, to thin.

2. Heat a medium nonstick skillet over medium-high heat. Add 3 tablespoons of batter, swirling it around to coat the entire pan. Cook for 1 to 2 minutes, then loosen the edges with a spatula or knife and flip the crepe. Cook for 1 minute and transfer to a plate. Repeat with the remaining batter.

3. To assemble, lay one crepe flat on a plate and add 6 to 8 banana and strawberry slices down one side. Fold the crepe in half. Repeat with a second crepe on the same plate. Drizzle chocolate sauce over them and dust with powdered sugar, if using. Repeat with remaining crepes.

VARIATION TIP: For savory crepes, swap the sugar for ½ teaspoon each salt and pepper and add fresh or dried herbs. Then fill the crepes with a savory stuffing, like roasted grape tomatoes and spinach or asparagus and vegan Cheddar-style shreds.

Good Morning Sunshine Smoothie

SERVES
2

PREP TIME
5 MINUTES

PER SERVING

CALORIES:
314

TOTAL FAT:
4 G

CARBS:
70 G

FIBER:
10 G

PROTEIN:
6 G

CALCIUM:
527 MG

VITAMIN D:
101 MCG

VITAMIN B12:
0 MCG

IRON:
2 MG

ZINC:
1 MG

Smoothies are an excellent way to get a couple of servings of fresh fruit at the start of your day. They take almost no time to prepare, which makes them a great on-the-go meal for busy mornings. I recommend freezing fruit ahead of time to make these easy to throw together. To pack your smoothie with protein, add 1 to 2 tablespoons of ground flaxseed, hemp, chia seeds, or a vegan protein powder.

3 sliced bananas, frozen
2 cups sliced frozen strawberries
½ cup frozen raspberries

1 cup orange juice
2 cups almond milk

Combine the bananas, strawberries, raspberries, orange juice, and almond milk in a high-speed blender (or a regular blender with an ice-crush setting). Blend until smooth.

PREP TIP: To make your morning smoothie prep even faster, prep over the weekend: Divide your frozen fruit into smoothie-size portions and freeze them in freezer-safe bags. In the morning, grab a bag and add it to a blender with orange juice and almond milk for a quick, nutritious breakfast to go!

Blueberry Chai Smoothie

SERVES
2

PREP TIME
10 MINUTES

I first tried a chai smoothie in a restaurant years ago, and it's been a favorite of mine ever since. Chai means "tea" in India, and masala chai is a black tea that is brewed with spices such as cinnamon, ginger, cardamom, and cloves. Masala chai mixture, sometimes labeled just "chai," has gained popularity in North America, so you should be able to find it at your local grocery store in the coffee and tea or international foods section.

3 sliced bananas, frozen

1 cup sliced frozen strawberries

2 cups frozen blueberries

1 cup masala chai, brewed

2 cups almond milk

Combine the bananas, strawberries, blueberries, chai, and almond milk in a high-speed blender (or a regular blender with an ice-crush setting). Blend until smooth.

VARIATION TIP: If you can't find chai tea, replace it with an additional cup of almond milk and 1 teaspoon ground cinnamon, ½ teaspoon ground nutmeg, and ¼ teaspoon ground ginger. Though not exactly chai, it will give your smoothie a similar warm undertone.

PER SERVING

CALORIES:
302

TOTAL FAT:
4 G

CARBS:
69 G

FIBER:
10 G

PROTEIN:
5 G

CALCIUM:
503 MG

VITAMIN D:
101 MCG

VITAMIN B12:
0 MCG

IRON:
2 MG

ZINC:
1 MG

Fruit Explosion Muffins

MAKES
12 MUFFINS

PREP TIME
5 MINUTES

COOK TIME
20 MINUTES

PER SERVING

CALORIES:
132

TOTAL FAT:
1 G

CARBS:
26 G

FIBER:
4 G

PROTEIN:
4 G

CALCIUM:
86 MG

VITAMIN D:
0 MCG

VITAMIN B12:
0 MCG

IRON:
2 MG

ZINC:
0 MG

These muffins get their name because they explode with fresh fruit flavor. When they're in season, I use mixed berries, but you can use whatever fruit is fresh and abundant. Apple and banana work really well together, as do blackberries and peaches. For earthier, nuttier muffins, I sometimes use whole wheat flour in place of all-purpose flour. I prefer large-flake oats for their extra hearty texture, but small-flake or quick-cooking oats will give you the same flavor.

1 cup fresh blueberries

1 cup fresh raspberries

½ cup sliced strawberries

2 teaspoons granulated sugar

1½ cups, plus 2 teaspoons
  all-purpose or whole wheat flour

1 tablespoon ground flaxseed

3 tablespoons hot water

1 cup rolled oats

1 tablespoon baking powder

¼ teaspoon salt

¼ teaspoon ground cinnamon

1 cup unsweetened soy milk

¼ cup packed brown sugar

¼ cup unsweetened applesauce

1 teaspoon vanilla extract

1. Preheat the oven to 350°F. Grease or line a 12-cup muffin tin.

2. In a large bowl, combine the blueberries, raspberries, and strawberries. Toss with the sugar and 2 teaspoons of flour. Set aside.

3. In a small bowl, mix the ground flaxseed with the hot water and stir. Set aside to let it thicken for 5 minutes.

4. In a second large bowl, sift together the remaining 1½ cups of flour, the oats, baking powder, salt, and cinnamon. Add the flaxseed egg, soy milk, brown sugar, applesauce, and vanilla extract. Stir gently until just combined. Gently fold in the berry mixture.

5. Using a large ice cream scoop, fill each muffin tin ¾ full. Bake for 20 minutes or until a toothpick inserted in the center of a muffin comes out clean. Serve warm or store in an airtight container for 2 to 3 days.

TECHNIQUE TIP: Coating the berries in sugar and flour keeps them from settling at the bottom of the batter and helps ensure every bite is fruit-filled. For some extra crunch and texture, sprinkle some coarse sugar on top of the muffins before putting them in the oven.

Creamy Cauliflower Soup

SERVES
6 TO 8

PREP TIME
15 MINUTES

COOK TIME
20 MINUTES

This is a hearty, comforting soup for a winter lunch or dinner. This recipe makes a lot of soup, so you can serve it to a crowd or make it a "stretch meal" and freeze some of it for another time. To make this soup over-the-top rich and delicious, add 1 cup of vegan Cheddar- or Monterey Pepper Jack-style shreds to the milk while it's simmering, stirring constantly until melted.

2 tablespoons extra-virgin olive oil
½ medium onion, diced
1 carrot, diced small
2 celery stalks, diced small
1 large head cauliflower, cut
   into florets
2½ cups water
1 vegetable bouillon cube

3 tablespoons all-purpose flour
1 teaspoon salt
½ teaspoon ground black pepper
½ teaspoon ground cumin
½ teaspoon onion powder
⅛ teaspoon ground nutmeg
3 tablespoons vegan butter
2 cups unsweetened soy milk

PER SERVING

CALORIES:
150

TOTAL FAT:
9 G

CARBS:
13 G

FIBER:
4 G

PROTEIN:
6 G

CALCIUM:
49 MG

VITAMIN D:
0 MCG

VITAMIN B12:
0 MCG

IRON:
1 MG

ZINC:
1 MG

1. In a large pot, heat the olive oil over medium-high heat. Add the onion, carrot, and celery, and sauté until the onion is translucent, about 5 minutes.

2. Add the cauliflower, water, and vegetable bouillon. Bring to a boil, then reduce heat and simmer for 12 to 15 minutes or until the cauliflower is tender.

3. In a small dish, combine the flour, salt, pepper, cumin, onion powder, and nutmeg. Set aside.

4. In a medium saucepan, melt the butter over medium-high heat. Add the flour mixture and stir constantly with a mixing spoon until combined. Switch to a wire whisk and slowly add the milk, whisking constantly to combine. Simmer until thickened, about 2 minutes.

5. Pour the milk mixture into the large pot with the cauliflower. Stir to combine. Working in small batches, purée the soup in a blender (or use an immersion blender) until it is thick and creamy and no chunks remain. Ladle into bowls and serve.

STRETCH TIP: If you have stale bread lying around, you can make croutons to serve with this soup. Cube the bread and toss with olive oil, salt, and pepper and bake for 15 minutes at 350°F.

Potato Corn Chowder

SERVES
6

PREP TIME
15 MINUTES

COOK TIME
30 MINUTES

PER SERVING

CALORIES:
309

TOTAL FAT:
15 G

CARBS:
38 G

FIBER:
5 G

PROTEIN:
7 G

CALCIUM:
33 MG

VITAMIN D:
0 MCG

VITAMIN B12:
1 MCG

IRON:
2 MG

ZINC:
0 MG

This is one of my all-time favorite soups. It's chunky, creamy, hearty, and easy to customize. At its core, it's a delicious potato and corn soup. Jazzed up, it's a party in a bowl. You can easily turn this soup into a loaded baked potato soup by mixing in 1 cup of vegan Cheddar-style shreds after it's blended and topping it with Smoky Tofu "Bacon" (page 18), a dollop of vegan sour cream, and diced chives.

2 tablespoons extra-virgin olive oil

1 medium onion, diced

1 carrot, diced

2 celery stalks, diced

2 garlic cloves, minced

4 to 5 yellow potatoes, peeled and diced

2½ cups vegetable broth

1 (14-ounce) can coconut milk

2 cups frozen corn

2 tablespoons nutritional yeast

¼ to ½ teaspoon red pepper flakes

½ teaspoon paprika

1. In a large soup pot or Dutch oven, heat the oil over medium-high heat. Add the onion, carrot, and celery, and cook until the onions are translucent, about 5 minutes. Add the garlic and potatoes and cook for 7 to 10 minutes, or until the potatoes are fork tender.

2. Add the vegetable broth, coconut milk, and corn. Bring to a boil before reducing heat and simmering for 15 minutes. Add the nutritional yeast, red pepper flakes, and paprika, and cook for 2 minutes.

3. Working in small batches, purée half the soup in a blender (or use an immersion blender to purée it partially) and return it to the pot, leaving the other half chunky. Serve hot.

VARIATION TIP: Boost your veggie intake by adding 2 cups of frozen mixed vegetables to turn this soup into a hearty mixed vegetable chowder. Carrots, peas, green or wax beans, and broccoli work. Add them at the very end after you've pureed the soup, and simmer for 2 to 3 minutes, just until they're warmed through.

Roasted Mixed Pepper and Balsamic Chickpea Spread Sandwich

SERVES
2 TO 3

PREP TIME
15 MINUTES

COOK TIME
20 MINUTES

I love the bright, bold flavors in this sandwich—it's a great way to showcase the full flavor of chickpeas. The roasted peppers and onions add delicious sweetness, and the balsamic vinegar and sriracha add a one-two flavor punch. I like using vegan mozzarella-style slices to add creaminess, but this sandwich still tastes amazing without them. You can also add some baby spinach or arugula leaves for more texture and flavor.

PER SERVING

CALORIES:
870

TOTAL FAT:
26 G

CARBS:
134 G

FIBER:
19 G

PROTEIN:
31 G

CALCIUM:
376 MG

VITAMIN D:
0 MCG

VITAMIN B12:
0 MCG

IRON:
9 MG

ZINC:
3 MG

For the chickpea spread

1 (16-ounce) can chickpeas, drained and rinsed

1 avocado, sliced

¼ to ½ teaspoon sriracha or other hot sauce

2 tablespoons balsamic vinegar

1 teaspoon garlic powder

1 teaspoon onion powder

½ teaspoon salt

1 teaspoon ground black pepper

For the sandwiches

1 red bell pepper, cut into wide slices

1 yellow bell pepper, cut into wide slices

1 orange bell pepper, cut into wide slices

½ red onion, sliced into wide rings

2 tablespoons extra-virgin olive oil

½ teaspoon salt, divided

½ teaspoon ground black pepper, divided

3 to 4 vegan mozzarella-style slices, cut in half

2 to 3 small baguettes, sliced in half lengthwise

TO MAKE THE CHICKPEA SPREAD

In a large bowl, combine the chickpeas, avocado, sriracha, balsamic vinegar, garlic powder, onion powder, and salt and pepper. Using a fork or a potato masher, mash until the chickpeas are flaky.

CONTINUED >

Roasted Mixed Pepper and Balsamic Chickpea Spread Sandwich, CONTINUED

TO MAKE THE SANDWICHES

1. Preheat the oven to 400°F and line a large rimmed baking sheet with parchment paper. Spread the sliced peppers and onion out, on the baking sheet in a single layer and drizzle them with olive oil, salt, and pepper. Toss to coat. Roast for 20 minutes or until soft. Remove from the oven and allow to cool.

2. Spread the chickpea mash evenly across the bottom half of each baguette. Add a single layer of mozzarella slices, then top with roasted peppers and onion. Top the sandwich with the remaining bread.

PREP TIP: Since they take longer to cook, try roasting the peppers and onions ahead of time and refrigerate them in an airtight container for up to 4 days. This way, you can speed up your prep time for lunch by making the chickpea mash only.

Roasted Spicy Sweet Potato, Cranberry, and Kale Salad

SERVES
3 TO 4

PREP TIME
10 MINUTES

COOK TIME
25 MINUTES

I love the simplicity of this salad. It's bright, fresh, and packed with fiber and protein. The dried cranberries add lovely tartness to balance out the dish. To elevate this salad, swap regular pecans for candied pecans: In a large skillet over medium heat, melt ¼ cup brown sugar, ¼ teaspoon salt, ¼ teaspoon cinnamon, and 2 tablespoons water. Toss in the pecans and stir for 3 minutes, until candied. Remove from the pan and cool completely.

PER SERVING

CALORIES:
608

TOTAL FAT:
33 G

CARBS:
75 G

FIBER:
14 G

PROTEIN:
9 G

CALCIUM:
290 MG

VITAMIN D:
0 MCG

VITAMIN B12:
1 MCG

IRON:
4 MG

ZINC:
2 MG

3 large sweet potatoes, peeled and cubed

2 tablespoons extra-virgin olive oil

1 teaspoon salt

1 teaspoon ground black pepper

½ cup Lemon Tahini Vinaigrette (page 34)

1 (10-ounce) bag chopped kale (or 1 large bunch kale, stemmed and chopped)

½ cup pecan halves

1 cup dried large cranberries

1. Preheat the oven to 425°F. Line a large rimmed baking sheet with parchment paper. Spread the sweet potatoes out on the baking sheet in a single layer. Drizzle with the olive oil, salt, and pepper, and toss to coat. Bake for 20 to 25 minutes or until the potatoes are soft and slightly darkened. Set aside to cool.

2. While the potatoes cook, prepare the Lemon Tahini Vinaigrette.

3. In a large bowl, combine the kale, pecans, and cranberries. Toss with the vinaigrette and roasted sweet potatoes.

VARIATION TIP: If you can't find fresh kale, try swapping it for baby spinach or a spinach-arugula mix. Any dark leafy green will add great texture and flavor to this salad. You can also swap out the sweet potato for butternut squash.

Sweet and Spicy Rice and Vegetable Bowl

SERVES
3

PREP TIME
10 MINUTES

COOK TIME
15 MINUTES

PER SERVING

CALORIES:
617

TOTAL FAT:
30 G

CARBS:
75 G

FIBER:
9 G

PROTEIN:
14 G

CALCIUM:
141 MG

VITAMIN D:
0 MCG

VITAMIN B12:
0 MCG

IRON:
3 MG

ZINC:
2 MG

This recipe uses *inari age*, which are deep-fried tofu pockets often seen served stuffed with rice at sushi restaurants. Inari age can be found for a reasonable price at most Asian supermarkets. If you can't find it, you can use my Smoky Tofu "Bacon" (page 18) or a store-bought package of smoked tofu, sliced.

¼ cup Easy 4-Ingredient Vegan Mayonnaise (page 21)

2 tablespoons sriracha

3 cups cooked jasmine rice

1 cup fried bean curd, sliced

1 large mango, diced

2 avocados, pitted and sliced

1 carrot, shredded

1 seedless cucumber, sliced into half moons

1 package shredded, dried, roasted seaweed (or 1 to 2 roasted seaweed snack packages)

3 tablespoons soy sauce, divided

3 tablespoons sesame seeds, divided

2 scallions, finely chopped

1. Prepare the Easy 4-Ingredient Vegan Mayonnaise.

2. Place the mayonnaise and sriracha in a small bowl. Whisk until combined.

3. Place 1 cup of the cooked rice into a shallow, wide bowl. Layer with the bean curd, mango, avocado slices, shredded carrot, cucumber, and seaweed. Drizzle with the sriracha mayonnaise and 1 tablespoon of soy sauce. Sprinkle with 1 tablespoon of sesame seeds and scallions. Repeat for the other two bowls.

VARIATION TIP: Mix up your bowl by adding or substituting ingredients like leftover Spicy Tofu "Crab" Salad (page 49), Spicy Ginger Tofu (page 52), or Seasoned Breaded Tofu Cutlets (page 56). You can also add salad greens (in addition to or in place of the rice) and add different vegetables.

Avocado Superfood Salad

SERVES
4

PREP TIME
15 MINUTES

This salad is a powerhouse of nutrition and flavor. It's a great weekday lunch that takes minutes to assemble and keeps you going all day. Make the Vegan Caesar Dressing and Smoky Tofu "Bacon" in advance for a quick salad assembly. If you've got some day-old or almost stale bread hanging around, you can make your own croutons (see Stretch Tip on page 101).

1 cup Smoky Tofu "Bacon" (page 18)

1 cup Vegan Caesar Dressing (page 33)

1 head romaine or butter lettuce, chopped

1 (10-ounce) package chopped kale (or 1 large bunch kale, stemmed and chopped)

1 (10-ounce) package shaved brussels sprouts

1½ cups cooked edamame, shelled (see Technique Tip)

1 red bell pepper, sliced into 2-inch strips

2 cups croutons (see Stretch Tip in Creamy Cauliflower Soup on page 101)

2 ripe avocados, diced

½ cup sunflower seeds

PER SERVING

CALORIES:
764

TOTAL FAT:
52 G

CARBS:
57 G

FIBER:
22 G

PROTEIN:
30 G

CALCIUM:
338 MG

VITAMIN D:
4 MCG

VITAMIN B12:
1 MCG

IRON:
7 MG

ZINC:
3 MG

1. Prepare the Smoky Tofu "Bacon" and Vegan Caesar Dressing.

2. In a large salad bowl, combine the lettuce, kale, sprouts, edamame, red bell pepper, tofu "bacon," and croutons. Toss with Caesar dressing. Top with diced avocado and sunflower seeds.

TECHNIQUE TIP: You should be able to find shelled edamame in the frozen vegetables section of your local grocery store. Cooking edamame is very simple—it just needs to steam for a couple of minutes in the microwave or on the stove in a double boiler over an inch or two of simmering water. Sprinkle edamame with a pinch of coarse salt once cooked to bring out its flavor.

Mushroom and Onion Pie

SERVES
3 TO 4

PREP TIME
10 MINUTES

COOK TIME
45 MINUTES

PER SERVING

CALORIES:
395

TOTAL FAT:
27 G

CARBS:
33 G

FIBER:
5 G

PROTEIN:
11 G

CALCIUM:
47 MG

VITAMIN D:
1 MCG

VITAMIN B12:
2 MCG

IRON:
2 MG

ZINC:
2 MG

This is a fabulous pie to serve alongside a salad for dinner. The mushrooms give it a rich, almost meaty flavor, but it's also slightly sweet as a result of the caramelized onions. If you don't have access to premade frozen puff pastry, use the crust recipe for Roasted Vegetable Pot Pie (page 119). To elevate this pie further, try adding diced zucchini or peas and carrots.

3 tablespoons extra-virgin olive oil

4 to 5 medium onions, thinly sliced

6 ounces cremini or button mushrooms, stemmed and thinly sliced (about 2 cups)

2 garlic cloves, minced

1 teaspoon dried thyme

½ teaspoon salt

½ teaspoon ground black pepper

1 cup vegetable stock

2 tablespoons all-purpose flour

¼ cup nutritional yeast

¼ cup fresh flat-leaf parsley, chopped

1 package vegan puff pastry (2 sheets), thawed

1. Preheat the oven to 350°F and grease a 10-inch pie dish.

2. In a large pan or Dutch oven, heat the oil over medium-high heat. Add the onions and mushrooms and cook until the onions are golden and the mushrooms are dark, stirring occasionally to cook evenly, about 10 minutes. Add the garlic, thyme, salt, and pepper, and cook for 1 minute.

3. Add the vegetable stock, flour, nutritional yeast, and parsley. Cook, stirring constantly, until the flour is dissolved and the mixture thickens. Set aside to cool slightly.

4. Unroll one sheet of puff pastry and line the pie dish with it, pressing the pastry gently into the bottom of the pan and up the sides. Trim off any excess. Spoon in the onion and mushroom filling and cover with the second sheet of puff pastry. Trim off any excess, and, using your fingers or a fork, press the edges down to seal the pie all around the circumference. Use a knife to make two crisscross slits in the center of the pie (to allow steam to escape while cooking). Cover the dish with aluminum foil and bake for 20 minutes. Remove the foil and bake for 10 minutes or until the puff pastry is golden. Serve hot.

BBQ Pulled Jackfruit Sandwiches

SERVES
4

PREP TIME
10 MINUTES

COOK TIME
15 MINUTES

Jackfruit is a tree fruit native to South and Southeast Asia whose flesh bears an uncanny resemblance to shredded pork. In recent years, it has gained popularity as a plant-based replacement for pulled pork. You can buy presliced and peeled canned jackfruit at most Asian supermarkets or online. Try to find jackfruit packed in water instead of brine—if you can find it only brine-packed, rinse it well before using.

PER SERVING

CALORIES:
639

TOTAL FAT:
27 G

CARBS:
95 G

FIBER:
8 G

PROTEIN:
9 G

CALCIUM:
229 MG

VITAMIN D:
0 MCG

VITAMIN B12:
0 MCG

IRON:
4 MG

ZINC:
1 MG

For BBQ jackfruit

1 cup Homemade BBQ Sauce
  (page 24)
2 (14-ounce) cans young jackfruit
  packed in water, drained
2 tablespoons extra-virgin
  olive oil
1 medium onion, diced
½ teaspoon salt
½ teaspoon ground
  black pepper

For the slaw and sandwiches

½ cup Easy 4-Ingredient Vegan
  Mayonnaise (page 21)
2 tablespoons granulated sugar
1½ tablespoons lemon juice
1 tablespoon white vinegar
½ teaspoon ground black pepper
¼ teaspoon salt
1 (8-ounce) bag shredded cabbage
  or coleslaw mix
4 hamburger buns

TO MAKE THE BBQ JACKFRUIT

1. Prepare the Homemade BBQ Sauce and Easy 4-Ingredient Vegan Mayonnaise.

2. Using your fingers, shred the drained jackfruit into a large bowl. Set aside.

3. In a wide skillet, heat the oil over medium-high heat. Add the onion and cook for 6 to 8 minutes, until translucent and golden. Add the shredded jackfruit, BBQ sauce, salt, and pepper. Stir until the jackfruit is warmed through and the sauce is bubbling, about 8 minutes.

CONTINUED >

BBQ Pulled Jackfruit Sandwiches, **CONTINUED**

TO MAKE THE SLAW AND SANDWICHES

1. While the jackfruit is cooking, prepare the Easy 4-Ingredient Vegan Mayonnaise.

2. Combine the mayonnaise, sugar, lemon juice, vinegar, pepper, and salt in a large bowl, and whisk until blended. Add the shredded cabbage and toss to coat.

3. Serve the BBQ jackfruit on a hamburger bun topped with coleslaw.

VARIATION TIP: You can use leftover BBQ jackfruit as a filling for tacos. Serve in flour tortillas topped with avocado, hot sauce, vegan Cheddar-style shreds, and cilantro.

Chorizo-Stuffed Peppers with Rice

SERVES
6

PREP TIME
10 MINUTES

COOK TIME
40 MINUTES

Stuffed peppers are always a hit in my house, mostly because they're a dish in an edible bowl—so much fun to eat! I have a habit of making too much rice, so I created this dish to use up leftovers from the night before. I like the heat from the Tofu Chorizo Crumble, but if you want to make a milder version, use the Meaty Tofu Crumble (page 17) instead.

2 cups Tofu Chorizo Crumble (page 16)

2 tablespoons extra-virgin olive oil

1 large onion, diced

5 large cremini mushrooms, stemmed and caps diced (about 1 cup)

½ green bell pepper, diced

3 cups cooked basmati rice

2 cups tomato sauce

2 teaspoons Italian or pizza seasoning

½ teaspoon salt

½ teaspoon ground black pepper

6 whole bell peppers (red, orange, or yellow), caps, stems, and ribs removed

1 cup vegan cheese shreds of choice

PER SERVING

CALORIES:
319

TOTAL FAT:
14 G

CARBS:
42 G

FIBER:
6 G

PROTEIN:
11 G

CALCIUM:
338 MG

VITAMIN D:
0 MCG

VITAMIN B12:
0 MCG

IRON:
4 MG

ZINC:
2 MG

1. Prepare the Tofu Chorizo Crumble. Preheat the oven to 400°F.

2. In a deep pan, heat the oil over medium-high heat. Sauté the onion until soft, about 5 minutes. Add the mushrooms and bell pepper and cook until they are golden and lightly caramelized, about 7 minutes.

3. Add the tofu chorizo, cooked rice, tomato sauce, Italian seasoning, salt, and pepper. Stir to combine. Simmer for 10 minutes, or until most of the sauce is absorbed by the rice.

4. Arrange the peppers standing up in a 9- by-11-inch baking dish. Fill each pepper with the chorizo and rice stuffing. Top with shredded cheese.

5. Bake uncovered for 20 minutes or until the cheese is melted and the peppers are soft.

PREP TIP: This is a great meal to make ahead and stash until needed. Simply prep the recipe up to step 4, then cover with foil and refrigerate until you're ready to cook.

Sweet and Spicy Cauliflower

SERVES
3 TO 4

PREP TIME
10 MINUTES

COOK TIME
20 MINUTES

PER SERVING

CALORIES:
328

TOTAL FAT:
15 G

CARBS:
36 G

FIBER:
9 G

PROTEIN:
16 G

CALCIUM:
137 MG

VITAMIN D:
0 MCG

VITAMIN B12:
0 MCG

IRON:
4 MG

ZINC:
2 MG

This recipe is a play on a dish I love from a local Chinese restaurant: crispy beef. I swapped out the fried beef for battered, oven-baked cauliflower and created a sauce that is sweet, spicy, and sticky but low in salt and sugar. You can eat this plain, on rice noodles, or with a side of rice.

2 tablespoons extra-virgin olive oil, divided
1 cup chickpea flour
½ teaspoon salt
½ teaspoon baking powder
1¼ cups unsweetened soy milk
1 large head cauliflower, cut into florets
½ cup soy sauce

1 tablespoon maple syrup
¼ cup rice vinegar
2 teaspoons sesame oil
2 teaspoons grated ginger
2 garlic cloves, minced
1 teaspoon sriracha
2 tablespoons cornstarch
¼ cup cold water
2 tablespoons sesame seeds

1. Preheat the oven to 450°F. Line a large rimmed baking sheet with parchment paper and brush lightly with 1 tablespoon of oil.

2. Make the battered cauliflower. In a small bowl, combine the chickpea flour, salt, and baking powder. Pour in the soy milk and stir to form a batter. Dip the cauliflower florets in the batter, shaking off any excess, and place in a single layer on the prepared baking sheet. Bake for 10 minutes.

3. Make the sauce. In a small saucepan, combine the soy sauce, maple syrup, rice vinegar, sesame oil, ginger, garlic, and sriracha, and bring to a simmer over medium heat.

4. In a small bowl, whisk together the cornstarch and water until the cornstarch is dissolved. Add this mixture to the saucepan and stir until thickened, about 2 minutes.

5. Remove the cauliflower from the oven, flip the florets over, and brush with the remaining 1 tablespoon of oil. Bake for 5 minutes. Transfer the cauliflower to a large bowl.

6. Pour the sauce over the cauliflower, tossing gently to coat. Return it to the baking sheet and bake for 5 more minutes. Remove from the oven and sprinkle with sesame seeds. Serve hot.

VARIATION TIP: Switch up the cauliflower for broccoli or go half and half to add a different texture to this dish. You can also use extra-firm tofu here too.

Roasted Veg Ratatouille on Creamy Polenta

SERVES
4

PREP TIME
15 MINUTES

COOK TIME
30 MINUTES

PER SERVING

CALORIES:
451

TOTAL FAT:
24 G

CARBS:
52 G

FIBER:
12 G

PROTEIN:
10 G

CALCIUM:
132 MG

VITAMIN D:
1 MCG

VITAMIN B12:
1 MCG

IRON:
3 MG

ZINC:
2 MG

Ratatouille is a wonderful vegetable dish from Provence, France. It is made in large batches to use up vegetables and is stewed in tomatoes and red wine to give it a bold flavor. This quick version uses the oven to roast the vegetables, which saves time and adds a wonderful caramelized taste. Because polenta hardens once cooled, you should make it close to serving time.

1 small eggplant, skin on, cubed
5 tablespoons extra-virgin olive
  oil, divided
1 teaspoon salt, divided
1 red onion, cut into chunks
1 green zucchini, diced large
1 yellow zucchini, diced large
6 ounces cremini mushrooms,
  thinly sliced (about 2 cups)

1 red bell pepper, diced large
1 recipe Creamy Polenta
  (page 130)
2 garlic cloves, sliced
1 (28-ounce) can diced
  tomatoes, drained
½ teaspoon dried oregano
½ teaspoon dried basil
½ teaspoon dried thyme

1. Preheat the oven to 425°F. Line two large rimmed baking sheets with parchment paper. Spread the eggplant on one baking sheet in a single layer. Drizzle with 2 tablespoons of olive oil and ½ teaspoon of salt. Toss to coat.

2. Spread the red onion, zucchini, mushrooms, and bell pepper on the second baking sheet. Toss with 1 tablespoon of olive oil and the remaining ½ teaspoon salt. Place both racks in the oven, eggplant on the lower rack, and bake for 20 minutes.

3. While the vegetables roast, prepare the polenta.

4. In a large pot, heat the remaining 2 tablespoons of oil over medium-high heat. Add the garlic and cook, stirring constantly, for 2 minutes. Add the tomatoes, oregano, basil, and thyme. Stir to combine. Simmer for 5 to 10 minutes.

5. Remove both trays from oven, toss the vegetables, and return to the oven, moving the eggplant to the upper rack. Bake for 5 to 10 minutes or until the eggplant is golden and the pepper and onion are caramelized and soft.

6. Remove the trays from the oven and add the vegetables to the pot. Stir to combine. Remove from heat and serve on top of the polenta.

TECHNIQUE TIP: Got an open bottle of red wine lying around? Add a splash of it to the diced tomatoes and herbs while they simmer. It adds a deep flavor and color.

Sweet Potato Crisp

SERVES
6 TO 8

PREP TIME
15 MINUTES

COOK TIME
40 MINUTES

PER SERVING

CALORIES:
106

TOTAL FAT:
4 G

CARBS:
16 G

FIBER:
3 G

PROTEIN:
1 G

CALCIUM:
31 MG

VITAMIN D:
0 MCG

VITAMIN B12:
0 MCG

IRON:
0 MG

ZINC:
0 MG

I love making this dish for the holidays. It's been a crowd-pleaser among both omnivores and plant-based guests at my Thanksgiving table for a few years now. If preparing in advance, follow all the steps up to baking in step 3 and refrigerate it until you're ready to bake.

2 medium sweet potatoes, peeled and cubed

2 large carrots, peeled and diced

2 parsnips, peeled and diced

½ cup orange juice

1 tablespoon maple syrup

3 tablespoons vegan butter, divided

2 garlic cloves, minced

½ teaspoon salt

½ teaspoon ground black pepper

⅛ teaspoon ground nutmeg

½ teaspoon ground cinnamon

2 teaspoons dried thyme, divided

½ cup bread crumbs

¼ cup chopped pecans

1. Preheat the oven to 350°F. Lightly grease a 9-inch square baking dish. Combine the sweet potatoes, carrots, and parsnips in a large pot and add water to just cover the vegetables. Bring to a boil and cook for 10 to 15 minutes, until fork-tender. Drain and transfer to a food processor or blender.

2. Add the orange juice, maple syrup, 1 tablespoon of vegan butter, garlic cloves, salt, pepper, nutmeg, cinnamon, and 1 teaspoon of thyme to the food processor, and process until smooth. Transfer to the prepared baking dish.

3. Melt the remaining 2 tablespoons of butter in the microwave. Prepare the topping by combining bread crumbs, pecans, melted butter, and the remaining teaspoon of thyme in a bowl. Sprinkle this over the sweet potato mix in the baking dish. Cover the baking dish with foil and bake for 20 minutes. Remove the foil and bake for 5 to 10 minutes or until the topping is golden. Serve warm.

VARIATION TIP: Dice 1 large Granny Smith apple and add it to a food processor or blender with 1 cup of fresh or frozen cranberries, 1 tablespoon of brown sugar, and ¼ teaspoon of cinnamon. Pulse until chopped and add a layer in between the sweet potato mix and the topping.

Mushroom Teriyaki with Broccoli

SERVES
3 TO 4

PREP TIME
10 MINUTES

COOK TIME
15 MINUTES

Portobello mushrooms are a great way to add meaty flavor and texture to a plant-based dish. This dish uses sliced portobellos in place of beef for a delicious ode to Japanese beef teriyaki. I pair this with steamed broccoli, whose deep flavor stands up to the richness of the sauce. I like to serve it over rice or rice noodles.

PER SERVING

CALORIES:
185

TOTAL FAT:
7 G

CARBS:
26 G

FIBER:
4 G

PROTEIN:
8 G

CALCIUM:
47 MG

VITAMIN D:
0 MCG

VITAMIN B12:
0 MCG

IRON:
2 MG

ZINC:
0 MG

1½ cups Teriyaki Sauce (page 29)
1 head broccoli, cut into florets
2 tablespoons extra-virgin olive oil
½ medium onion, thinly sliced
2 scallions, finely chopped

2 garlic cloves, minced
6 large portobello mushroom caps, thickly sliced
1 red bell pepper, thinly sliced
Cooked rice or noodles, for serving

1. Prepare the Teriyaki Sauce.

2. Fill a large saucepan with 1 inch of water and bring to a boil. Add the broccoli florets, cover, and reduce heat to medium. Steam for 5 minutes. Remove the broccoli from the pot and set aside.

3. In a deep skillet, heat the olive oil over medium-high heat. Add the onion and scallions and cook for 3 to 4 minutes or until the onion is almost translucent. Add the garlic, portobello mushroom slices, and bell pepper, and cook for 4 to 5 minutes on each side, until the mushrooms are dark and golden.

4. Add the broccoli to the pan and pour in the Teriyaki Sauce. Toss to coat and cook until the sauce is warmed through, about 2 minutes. Serve with rice or noodles.

VARIATION TIP: Portobello mushrooms have a strong, earthy flavor. If you're looking for something milder, swap them out for cremini (baby portobello) mushrooms. You could also add some extra-firm tofu or fried bean curd (inari age).

Coconut Curry Vegetable Soup

A twist on regular vegetable soup, this dish uses fragrant curry paste and coconut milk to form a rich, creamy soup that is comforting on a cold day. It's a handy "clean out the fridge" dish that I like to make at the end of a week when I have leftover vegetables to use up. Frozen vegetables work well in this dish and reduce the amount of prep time.

1 heaping tablespoon Basic Curry Paste (page 20)
2 tablespoons extra-virgin olive oil
1 large onion, diced
1 large carrot, diced
2 celery stalks, diced
2 garlic cloves, minced
2 teaspoons grated ginger
1 tablespoon soy sauce

2 (14-ounce) cans coconut milk
2 cups vegetable broth
1 cup diced frozen butternut squash
2 cups frozen cauliflower florets
1 (15-ounce) can baby corn
1 cup frozen peas
Juice of ½ lime

1. Prepare the Basic Curry Paste.

2. In a large soup pot, heat the oil over medium-high heat. Add the onion, carrot, and celery, and cook for 5 to 7 minutes, until the onion is translucent and the carrot and celery are softened. Add the garlic, ginger, and curry paste, and cook, stirring constantly, for 1 minute until the curry paste is warm and fragrant.

3. Add the soy sauce, coconut milk, vegetable broth, butternut squash, and frozen cauliflower. Bring to a boil, then reduce heat to medium and simmer for 15 minutes, or until the frozen cauliflower is tender. Add the baby corn, frozen peas, and lime juice. Stir to combine. Remove from heat and serve.

VARIATION TIP: To save time, you can swap out the homemade curry paste for red Thai curry paste. Try tossing an 8-ounce package of rice noodles into the broth during the last 5 minutes of cooking.

Roasted Vegetable Pot Pie

SERVES
3 TO 4

PREP TIME
20 MINUTES

COOK TIME
30 MINUTES

This is a fun twist on a traditional pot pie. It's sort of a "cheater" pie because it has only pie crust on top, which reduces the cooking time significantly. If you want to make a full pie crust (top and bottom), double the crust ingredients and prebake the bottom shell for 15 minutes before filling it. Be sure to cut all the vegetables in similar sizes so the pie filling cooks evenly.

For the pie dough

1½ cups all-purpose flour

½ teaspoon salt

½ cup vegan butter

4 to 5 teaspoons cold water

For the pot pie

1 large red onion, chopped

1 zucchini, chopped

1 yellow squash, chopped

1 small head of broccoli, cut into
  small florets

2 tablespoons extra-virgin olive oil

2 tablespoons vegan butter

2 tablespoons all-purpose flour

2 cups unsweetened soy milk

1 vegetable bouillon cube

½ teaspoon salt

½ teaspoon dried oregano

½ teaspoon dried thyme

½ teaspoon ground black pepper

PER SERVING

CALORIES:
586

TOTAL FAT:
38 G

CARBS:
48 G

FIBER:
9 G

PROTEIN:
14 G

CALCIUM:
76 MG

VITAMIN D:
0 MCG

VITAMIN B12:
0 MCG

IRON: 4 MG

ZINC: 1 MG

TO MAKE THE PIE DOUGH

In a large bowl, combine the flour and salt. Using a pastry cutter or two knives, "cut" butter into the flour until the butter is the size of small peas. Add 4 teaspoons of water and mix and knead to form a dough. If the dough feels dry, add the remaining teaspoon of water. Wrap in plastic wrap and refrigerate for 15 minutes.

TO MAKE THE POT PIE

1. While the pie dough chills, preheat the oven to 425°F. Line a large baking sheet with parchment paper. Spread out the onion, zucchini, and broccoli in a single layer on the baking sheet. Drizzle with olive oil. Roast for 20 to 22 minutes.

2. In a deep pan, melt the 2 remaining tablespoons of butter. Add the remaining 2 tablespoons of flour and mix to form a paste. Slowly add the soy milk, stirring constantly until incorporated.

CONTINUED >

Roasted Vegetable Pot Pie, CONTINUED

3. Add the vegetable bouillon cube, remaining ½ teaspoon of salt, oregano, thyme, and pepper. Simmer for 5 minutes or until thickened enough to coat the back of a spoon. Add the roasted vegetables and toss to coat. Transfer the mixture to a 10-inch pie plate. Reduce the oven heat to 375°F.

4. Remove the pie dough from the plastic wrap and roll it out to a ½-inch-thick circle. Drape the dough over the top of the filled pie dish, trimming off the excess dough, and crimp the edges to form a seal, using your fingers or a fork. Cut an "x" slit on top of the pie crust and bake for 10 minutes or until the crust is golden.

STRETCH TIP: Double this recipe and make an extra pie to freeze (follow all steps except baking; freeze, and put it in the oven at 375°F for 30 minutes when you want it). Pot pies are great freezer meals and handy when you want a warm, comforting dish but don't feel like doing all that prep.

Cauliflower Wings Two Ways

SERVES
2 TO 3

PREP TIME
15 MINUTES

COOK TIME
30 MINUTES

These are straight-from-the-pub-style wings made healthier (and without the long wait for a table). Battered and baked cauliflower florets provide the perfect base for these wings, served two ways: with hot sauce and teriyaki. Serve these wings with celery and carrot sticks and a side of White Garlic Dill Sauce (page 27) for a real pub-like experience at home.

1½ cups Teriyaki Sauce (page 29)
½ cup unsweetened soy milk
½ cup water
¾ cup all-purpose flour
1 teaspoon onion powder
1 teaspoon garlic powder
¼ teaspoon salt

¼ teaspoon ground black pepper
1 large head cauliflower, cut
    into florets
⅓ cup vegan butter
½ cup thick hot sauce, such as
    Frank's Red Hot

PER SERVING

CALORIES:
798

TOTAL FAT:
58 G

CARBS:
58 G

FIBER:
10 G

PROTEIN:
13 G

CALCIUM:
97 MG

VITAMIN D:
0 MCG

VITAMIN B12:
0 MCG

IRON:
4 MG

ZINC:
1 MG

1. Prepare the Teriyaki Sauce.

2. Preheat the oven to 425°F. Line a large baking sheet with parchment paper. Set aside.

3. Make the battered cauliflower. In a shallow, wide dish, combine the soy milk, water, flour, onion powder, garlic powder, salt, and pepper to form a batter. Dip the cauliflower wings in the batter, allowing any excess to drip off. Place the cauliflower wings in a single layer on the prepared baking sheet and bake for 20 minutes, flipping halfway through.

4. Make the hot sauce mixture. Combine the butter and hot sauce in a small saucepan over medium heat. Simmer until the butter is melted. Remove from heat.

5. Remove the cauliflower wings from the oven and divide them evenly between two large bowls. Add the hot sauce mixture to one bowl and the Teriyaki Sauce to the other. Toss each bowl to coat the cauliflower evenly. Return the cauliflower wings to the baking sheet and bake for another 10 minutes, or until crispy. Serve immediately.

VARIATION TIP: If you're not a fan of hot sauce, you can switch it out for Homemade BBQ Sauce (page 24) to make BBQ-style cauliflower wings.

SOY-FREE

Eggplant Parmesan Sandwiches

Eggplant Parmesan is a wonderfully rich meal, but it can also take hours to make. I've reduced that time by creating a quick sandwich version that captures the signature flavors of eggplant parmesan: tomato sauce, melted mozzarella, and, of course, decadent breaded eggplant. To cut down on time, I've fried the eggplant, but you can also bake it at 400°F for 15 minutes.

1 cup bread crumbs
1 cup panko bread crumbs
2 tablespoons nutritional yeast
1 tablespoon dried oregano
1 tablespoon dried basil
1 tablespoon onion powder
½ teaspoon salt
½ teaspoon ground black pepper

1 (14-ounce) can coconut milk
3 tablespoons vegetable oil
2 medium eggplants, sliced into
   ¼-inch rounds
4 small baguettes or ciabatta buns,
   cut in half lengthwise
1½ cups tomato sauce
2 cups vegan mozzarella-style shreds

1. In a shallow bowl, combine the bread crumbs, panko crumbs, nutritional yeast, oregano, basil, onion powder, salt, and pepper. Pour the coconut milk into a second shallow bowl.

2. In a wide skillet, heat the vegetable oil over medium-high heat. In batches of 2 or 3 (depending on the size of the skillet), dip each side of the eggplant slices in the coconut milk and then in the breadcrumb mixture. Add to the skillet and fry for 2 to 3 minutes on each side or until golden. Transfer to a paper towel–lined plate and repeat with the remaining eggplant.

3. Preheat the oven to Broil. On a small rimmed baking sheet, space the bottom halves of the baguettes evenly apart.

4. Layer slices of the fried eggplant on each baguette. Spoon 2 to 3 tablespoons of tomato sauce over the eggplant and top with the mozzarella shreds. Place in the oven and broil for 3 to 4 minutes or until the cheese is melted.

5. Remove from the oven and top with the remaining tomato sauce and top halves of the baguettes. Serve immediately.

Curried Potato, Cauliflower, and Pea Burritos

SERVES
6

PREP TIME 15 MINUTES

COOK TIME
20 MINUTES

PER SERVING

CALORIES:
320

TOTAL FAT:
14 G

CARBS:
40 G

FIBER:
7 G

PROTEIN:
8 G

CALCIUM:
119 MG

VITAMIN D:
0 MCG

VITAMIN B12:
0 MCG

IRON:
3 MG

ZINC:
1 MG

This dish is a mashup of two of my favorites: burritos and samosas. I've created a mixture inspired by samosa fillings, stuffed it into a tortilla, and grilled it for a delicious and quick dinner. If you have a panini press, you can use that to press or toast your burritos instead.

2 tablespoons Basic Curry Paste (page 20)
2 large yellow potatoes, diced
1 large carrot, peeled and diced
2 cups cauliflower florets
2 tablespoons extra-virgin olive oil
1 medium onion, diced
2 garlic cloves, minced
1 cup frozen peas
1 cup canned coconut milk
6 large flour tortillas

1. Prepare the Basic Curry Paste. Next, place the potatoes, carrot, and cauliflower in a large pot and fill with enough water to cover the vegetables. Bring to a boil and cook until the vegetables are just tender, about 10 minutes. Drain and set aside.

2. In a deep skillet, heat the olive oil over medium-high heat. Add the onion and cook until translucent, about 5 minutes. Add the garlic and cook for 1 minute.

3. Add the cooked potatoes, carrot, cauliflower, frozen peas, and curry paste. Stir to combine. Add the coconut milk and simmer for 7 to 10 minutes, or until the sauce thickens and is mostly absorbed. Remove from heat.

4. Divide the filling between the tortillas. Roll each tortilla into a burrito by folding in the sides first, then folding up the bottom, tucking under as you roll toward the top.

5. Warm a dry skillet on medium-high heat and place the burritos, two at a time, in the skillet with the folded side down. Use a large spatula to press down on the burritos and cook for 2 minutes on each side. Serve hot.

Roasted Rainbow Veg with Pearl Couscous, 146

6

Grains: Quinoa, Millet, and More

Smoky Sweet Quinoa and Peppers

SERVES
6 TO 8

PREP TIME
15 MINUTES

COOK TIME
60 MINUTES

PER SERVING

CALORIES:
189

TOTAL FAT:
6 G

CARBS:
29 G

FIBER:
5 G

PROTEIN:
7 G

CALCIUM:
54 MG

VITAMIN D:
0 MCG

VITAMIN B12:
0 MCG

IRON:
2 MG

ZINC:
1 MG

This dish is inspired by paella, a Spanish dish made of rice, meat or seafood, and vegetables. I've created this quinoa variation to introduce a different texture and flavor and make vegetables the star of the show. When in season, consider swapping the green beans for fresh asparagus—its natural sweetness complements this dish's smoky undertones.

2 tablespoons extra-virgin olive oil
1 large sweet onion, diced
2 scallions, finely chopped
2 garlic cloves, diced
1 celery stalk, diced
1 red bell pepper, diced
1 orange bell pepper diced
1 yellow bell pepper, diced
1 teaspoon salt, divided
2 tablespoons tomato paste
2 cups green beans, sliced into
   ½-inch pieces

1½ cups uncooked quinoa
1 teaspoon paprika
¼ teaspoon black pepper
½ cup white wine (optional)
3 cups vegetable broth, divided
1 vegetable bouillon cube
½ cup water
¼ cup chopped parsley, for garnish
1 lemon, quartered, for garnish

1. Heat the olive oil in a deep pan over medium-high heat. Add the onion and scallions and cook until soft for about 5 minutes, stirring often.

2. Add the garlic, celery, bell peppers, and ½ teaspoon of salt. Cook for 15 minutes, stirring often.

3. Add the tomato paste and green beans. Cook 2 minutes.

4. Add the uncooked quinoa, paprika, remaining salt, and pepper. Cook for 3 to 4 minutes, stirring often, to incorporate the quinoa into the mixture.

5. Add the wine, if using, 1 cup of vegetable broth, and the bouillon cube, and bring to a boil. Immediately reduce the heat to low. Simmer uncovered for 25 minutes, stirring occasionally, adding the remaining 2 cups of broth one cup at a time, waiting until it is absorbed before adding more.

6. While the dish simmers, preheat the oven to 375°F. Once cooked, transfer the contents of the pan to a 9-by-13-inch baking dish.

7. Pour the water evenly over the dish and bake, uncovered, for 10 minutes.

8. Remove from the oven. Sprinkle with the chopped parsley and squeeze one lemon wedge over the dish. Garnish with the remaining lemon wedges. Serve immediately.

VARIATION TIP: Baking this dish for 10 minutes gives the quinoa a crunchy texture and a nuttier flavor, but to save time, skip the baking portion. The dish is fully cooked in step 5.

One-Pot Creamy Fusilli

SERVES
4

PREP TIME
5 MINUTES

COOK TIME
20 MINUTES

PER SERVING

CALORIES:
613

TOTAL FAT:
15 G

CARBS:
96 G

FIBER:
16 G

PROTEIN:
28 G

CALCIUM:
83 MG

VITAMIN D:
1 MCG

VITAMIN B12:
3 MCG

IRON:
6 MG

ZINC:
2 MG

One-pot meals are a great way to get a well-balanced dish on the table without spending a lot of time or using a lot of equipment. This pasta dish is a go-to for me on busy nights. It's rich and flavorful but not overbearingly tomato-ey (great for my kids, who don't love tomatoes). Cooking the pasta in the sauce saves time and allows the flavors to soak into the noodles.

3 tablespoons extra-virgin olive oil
1 large onion, chopped
4 ounces cremini or button mushrooms, stemmed and thinly sliced (about 1¼ cups)
1 zucchini, diced
3 cloves garlic, minced
¾ cup tomato paste
2 cups grape tomatoes, halved
½ teaspoon salt
¼ teaspoon ground black pepper

¼ teaspoon red pepper flakes
½ teaspoon dried oregano
½ teaspoon dried basil
1 vegetable bouillon cube
2 cups vegetable broth
1 cup unsweetened soy milk
½ cup water
1 (16-ounce) box fusilli noodles
⅓ cup nutritional yeast
¾ cup fresh baby spinach leaves

1. In a large pot with a tight-fitting lid, heat the oil on medium-high heat. Add the onion, mushrooms, and zucchini. Cook until the onion is translucent and the zucchini is softened, about 5 minutes.

2. Add the garlic and tomato paste and cook for 2 minutes.

3. Add the tomatoes, salt, black pepper, red pepper flakes, oregano, and basil, and cook until the tomatoes are wilted, about 5 minutes.

4. Add the bouillon cube, vegetable broth, milk, water, and fusilli. Bring to a boil, then immediately reduce heat to medium-low. Stir and cover, simmering for 10 to 12 minutes.

5. Stir in the nutritional yeast and spinach. Stir for 2 to 3 minutes or until the spinach has wilted. Serve hot.

VARIATION TIP: Boost the protein and fiber in this dish by adding one (15-ounce) can of drained and rinsed chickpeas to the pot along with the spinach and nutritional yeast.

Thai Red Curry Noodles with Eggplant

SERVES
3 TO 4

PREP TIME
10 MINUTES

COOK TIME
20 MINUTES

This dish is full of deep, aromatic flavor. The fresh ginger and red curry paste—which you can find at most grocery stores or online—add wonderful heat that balances perfectly with the rich coconut milk. While you may be tempted to use light coconut milk because of its lower fat content, don't do it for this dish. This recipe needs full-fat coconut milk to thicken the sauce and deepen the flavor.

1 (8-ounce) package rice noodles
2 tablespoons extra-virgin olive oil
1 medium onion, diced
1 medium eggplant, cubed
1 teaspoon grated ginger
1 teaspoon minced garlic

1 (15-ounce) can diced
   tomatoes, drained
1 tablespoon store-bought Thai red
   curry paste
1 (14-ounce) can coconut milk
3 scallions, finely chopped

PER SERVING

CALORIES:
366

TOTAL FAT:
22 G

CARBS:
35 G

FIBER:
8 G

PROTEIN:
5 G

CALCIUM:
66 MG

VITAMIN D:
0 MCG

VITAMIN B12:
0 MCG

IRON:
2 MG

ZINC:
0 MG

1. Cook the rice noodles according to package directions. Drain and set aside.

2. In a large skillet, heat the oil over medium-high heat. Add the onion and eggplant. Cook until the eggplant is soft, about 10 minutes.

3. Add the ginger and garlic. Cook for 1 minute.

4. Add the diced tomatoes and curry paste. Cook for 2 minutes, stirring constantly.

5. Add the coconut milk. Reduce heat to medium-low and simmer for 10 minutes to allow the sauce to thicken. Transfer the cooked rice noodles to the skillet and toss to coat them in the sauce. Garnish with the scallions before serving.

VARIATION TIP: Pack this dish full of vegetables by adding sliced carrots, baby corn, snow peas, and bamboo shoots. They add flavor, color, and texture, and you'll sneak in another serving of veggies in the process.

Creamy Polenta

SERVES
4

PREP TIME
5 MINUTES

COOK TIME
20 MINUTES

PER SERVING

CALORIES:
176

TOTAL FAT:
7 G

CARBS:
25 G

FIBER:
3 G

PROTEIN:
4 G

CALCIUM:
13 MG

VITAMIN D:
0 MCG

VITAMIN B12:
1 MCG

IRON:
1 MG

ZINC:
1 MG

Tired of the same old side dishes? Let's shake it up. Polenta is a creamy side dish that is a nice change from mashed potatoes or rice. It's delicious on its own or smothered with gravy or ratatouille. Like grits, polenta is made from cornmeal, but it has a slightly coarser texture. The key to making good polenta is keeping it lump-free, so use a good whisk and keep stirring.

2 cups water

2 cups vegetable broth

1 cup cornmeal

1 teaspoon salt

2 tablespoons vegan butter

½ teaspoon ground black pepper

2 tablespoons nutritional yeast

1 tablespoon unsweetened
   soy milk

1. Combine the water and broth in a medium saucepan and bring to a boil. Once boiling, add the cornmeal slowly, whisking constantly to ensure there are no lumps. Keep whisking for 1 to 2 minutes, or until the polenta has thickened. Add the salt.

2. Reduce heat to medium-low and let the polenta cook at a low bubble for about 20 minutes. Stir occasionally to prevent lumps from forming. Remove from the heat, and stir in the butter, pepper, nutritional yeast, and soy milk. Serve immediately.

STRETCH TIP: Refrigerate any leftover polenta. It will harden as it cools, which makes it perfect for quick and easy polenta cakes. Slice the hardened polenta and pan-fry it in olive oil or vegan butter for a crunchy-on-the-outside, soft-on-the-inside savory treat.

Bulgur and Chickpea Tabbouleh

SERVES
3 TO 4

PREP TIME
40 MINUTES

Tabbouleh is a vegetarian salad with origins in the Middle East and Mediterranean. It often consists of a grain mixed with parsley, mint, olive oil, and lemon. This recipe gives classic tabbouleh a twist by adding chickpeas, scallions, peppers, and vegetable broth for a fresh, bright, and savory flavor profile.

1¼ cups vegetable broth

1 cup bulgur

½ teaspoon salt

1 (15-ounce) can chickpeas, drained and rinsed

2 scallions, finely chopped

½ small red onion, finely diced

1 seedless cucumber, diced

1 red bell pepper, seeded and diced

2 cups grape tomatoes, halved

¼ cup fresh chopped dill

½ cup chopped fresh flat-leaf parsley

1 tablespoon lemon zest

Juice of 2 lemons

¼ cup extra-virgin olive oil

1 teaspoon sugar

1 garlic clove, minced

½ teaspoon ground black pepper

PER SERVING

CALORIES:
414

TOTAL FAT:
17 G

CARBS:
53 G

FIBER:
11 G

PROTEIN:
14 G

CALCIUM:
93 MG

VITAMIN D:
0 MCG

VITAMIN B12:
0 MCG

IRON:
2 MG

ZINC:
1 MG

1. Bring the vegetable broth to a boil in a small saucepan. Stir in the bulgur and salt, cover, and remove from the heat. Let it stand for 25 to 30 minutes, or until the broth is completely absorbed.

2. In a large bowl, combine the chickpeas, scallions, red onion, cucumber, red bell pepper, tomatoes, dill, and parsley. Add the cooked bulgur and stir to combine.

3. In a measuring glass, whisk together the lemon zest, lemon juice, olive oil, sugar, garlic, and pepper. Pour over the bulgur salad and toss to coat.

VARIATION TIP: This makes a great appetizer for a group. Cover a 10-inch round serving platter with a thick, even layer of hummus, then pile the bulgur salad in the middle of the plate. Drizzle with olive oil and hot sauce and garnish with lemon wedges. Serve with toasted pita chips.

Turmeric Millet with Cranberries, Raisins, and Almonds

SERVES
4

PREP TIME
5 MINUTES

COOK TIME
20 MINUTES

PER SERVING

CALORIES:
737

TOTAL FAT:
24 G

CARBS:
119 G

FIBER:
14 G

PROTEIN:
16 G

CALCIUM:
123 MG

VITAMIN D:
0 MCG

VITAMIN B12:
0 MCG

IRON:
5 MG

ZINC:
2 MG

This is my take on a couscous dish I grew up eating. Couscous is a pasta made from durum wheat semolina that contains gluten. To create this gluten-free recipe, I replaced couscous with millet, which is similar in shape and size to couscous. The turmeric in this dish gives the millet a striking yellow hue, and the cinnamon adds warmth to its flavor.

3 cups vegetable broth

1½ cups millet

2 tablespoons extra-virgin olive oil

½ medium onion, diced

1 cup sliced almonds

1 cup dried cranberries

1 cup golden raisins

¼ teaspoon ground turmeric

¼ teaspoon ground cinnamon

¼ teaspoon salt

½ teaspoon ground black pepper

1. In a medium pot with a tight-fitting lid, bring the vegetable broth to a boil. Add the millet and immediately reduce heat to low. Cover and simmer for 15 to 20 minutes, or until the broth is completely absorbed. Remove the lid and fluff with a fork.

2. While the millet is cooking, in a medium skillet, heat the olive oil over medium-high heat. Add the onions and cook for 7 to 10 minutes, until lightly golden. Remove the onions and set aside.

3. Reduce heat to medium and add the sliced almonds to the pan. Toast for 1 to 2 minutes, until fragrant but not browned.

4. Transfer the millet to a large bowl. Add the onions, almonds, cranberries, raisins, turmeric, cinnamon, salt, and pepper. Adjust salt and pepper as needed. Chill or serve immediately.

SUBSTITUTION TIP: For a nut-free version of this dish, swap the almonds for pumpkin or sunflower seeds. Be sure to toast them for a couple of minutes in a pan over medium heat to bring out their flavor.

Vegetable Barley Soup

SERVES
6

PREP TIME
15 MINUTES

COOK TIME
1 HOUR

Growing up, vegetable barley soup was a Sunday dinner staple. My mother made it from a popular kosher soup mix and added in whatever vegetables she had leftover in the house. Barley gives this soup a thick, rich, almost porridge-like consistency, and it warms you from the inside out. I've re-created the flavors of my mom's favorite mix in this large-batch soup. I hope it becomes one of your favorites, too.

2 tablespoons extra-virgin olive oil
1 medium onion, diced
2 carrots, peeled and diced
1 parsnip, peeled and diced
1 large yellow potato, peeled
   and diced
2 celery stalks, diced
3 garlic cloves, minced
2 tablespoons fresh dill, chopped

1 teaspoon dried thyme
½ teaspoon dried oregano
1 teaspoon salt
1 teaspoon ground black pepper
8 cups vegetable broth
1 cup water
2 cups barley
2 cups fresh baby spinach leaves

PER SERVING

CALORIES:
234

TOTAL FAT:
5 G

CARBS:
43 G

FIBER:
9 G

PROTEIN:
7 G

CALCIUM:
92 MG

VITAMIN D:
0 MCG

VITAMIN B12:
0 MCG

IRON:
2 MG

ZINC:
1 MG

1. In a large soup pot, heat the oil over medium-high heat. Add the onion, carrots, parsnip, potato, celery, and garlic. Cook for 10 to 12 minutes, stirring frequently until the onions are translucent and vegetables are softened.

2. Add the dill, thyme, oregano, salt, and pepper. Cook for 2 minutes, stirring frequently.

3. Pour in the vegetable broth, water, and barley. Bring it to a boil, then reduce heat to medium-low, cover, and simmer for about 1 hour, or until the barley is tender. Stir occasionally. If the soup seems too thick, add broth or water as needed. Adjust salt and pepper to taste. Remove from the heat, add the baby spinach, and stir until wilted, about 3 minutes. Serve hot.

STRETCH TIP: This soup freezes brilliantly, so even if you're not cooking for a crowd, make the full recipe and freeze it in batches. You'll be glad you did when it's cold outside and you want something quick, warm, and comforting.

Mushroom and Green Pea Farro Risotto

SERVES
4

PREP TIME
10 MINUTES

COOK TIME
40 MINUTES

PER SERVING

CALORIES:
259

TOTAL FAT:
8 G

CARBS:
36 G

FIBER:
6 G

PROTEIN:
12 G

CALCIUM:
58 MG

VITAMIN D:
2 MCG

VITAMIN B12:
2 MCG

IRON:
3 MG

ZINC:
2 MG

This dish, a twist on risotto, replaces the usual arborio rice with farro, an ancient grain high in protein. Farro comes in traditional or pearled versions. In pearled farro, the inedible hull is removed from the grain, making it much faster to cook than traditional farro. If you can't find pearled farro at your grocery store, use the traditional version here, but you'll need to double the simmering time.

2¼ cups vegetable broth
1 vegetable bouillon cube
2 tablespoons extra-virgin olive oil
½ cup onion, diced
2 scallions, finely chopped
2 garlic cloves, minced
8 ounces cremini mushrooms, stemmed and caps thinly sliced (about 2½ cups)

1 cup frozen peas
1 teaspoon dried thyme
1 teaspoon dried dill
½ teaspoon salt
½ teaspoon ground black pepper
1 cup pearled farro
¼ cup nutritional yeast

1. In a medium saucepan, combine the vegetable broth and bouillon cube. Bring it to a boil and remove from the heat. Set aside.

2. In a large, deep pot, heat the olive oil over medium-high heat. Add the onion, scallions, garlic, mushrooms, and frozen peas. Cook for 4 to 5 minutes.

3. Add the thyme, dill, salt, pepper, and farro to the pot. Cook for 5 minutes, allowing the farro to toast slightly.

4. Pour the broth into the farro mixture. Bring to a boil, then cover, reduce the heat to medium-low, and simmer for 20 to 30 minutes or until all the liquid is absorbed.

5. Remove from heat and stir in the nutritional yeast. Serve hot.

VARIATION TIP: This is a great base recipe for farro risotto that you can customize. When in season, try swapping out the frozen peas for fresh asparagus. Or, swap the dill for paprika and the peas for grape and sun-dried tomatoes.

Mixed Vegetable Fried Rice

SERVES
4 TO 6

PREP TIME
10 MINUTES

COOK TIME
20 MINUTES

This is a great dish to make when you have leftovers you need to use up—including rice! I constantly make far more rice than I need for a given meal, so I stash my leftovers in the fridge, and a day or two later, I make a batch of fried rice with it. This dish actually tends to work better with day-old rice, since it's a bit less sticky than fresh-cooked rice.

1 cup Smoky Tofu "Bacon"
   (page 18)
2 tablespoons extra-virgin olive oil
1 medium onion, diced
3 scallions, finely chopped, white
   and green parts separated
4 ounces cremini or button
   mushrooms, stemmed and caps
   thinly sliced

2 cups cooked jasmine or
   basmati rice
1 cup frozen mixed vegetables
   (peas, carrots, green beans)
1 cup frozen corn
¼ cup vegetable broth
¼ cup soy sauce

PER SERVING

CALORIES:
133

TOTAL FAT:
5 G

CARBS:
19 G

FIBER:
2 G

PROTEIN:
4 G

CALCIUM:
28 MG

VITAMIN D:
1 MCG

VITAMIN B12:
0 MCG

IRON:
1 MG

ZINC:
1 MG

1. Prepare the Smoky Tofu "Bacon." Then, in a large, deep pan, heat the olive oil over medium-high heat. Add the onion, white parts of the scallions, and mushrooms. Cook for 5 minutes, until the onions are translucent and soft, the scallions are fragrant, and the mushrooms are dark.

2. Add the cooked rice, frozen mixed vegetables, corn, vegetable broth, and soy sauce. Cook, stirring constantly, until all the rice is coated with the soy sauce and the vegetable stock has been absorbed. Top with tofu "bacon" and green parts of the scallions and serve.

STRETCH TIP: Almost any leftover vegetables you have in the fridge or freezer will work in this dish. Try adding broccoli, cauliflower, asparagus, or lima beans to the rice. If you want additional texture or crunch, try adding baby corn and water chestnuts.

Super Fruity Oat and Flaxseed Granola Bars

SERVES
8

PREP TIME
15 MINUTES
+ CHILL TIME

COOK TIME
10 MINUTES

I've always had hit-or-miss luck when it comes to granola bars. It's hard to find good vegan ones, and when you do find them, they are often crazy expensive. But since granola bars are an easy on-the-go breakfast or snack, I knew I had to come up with a version that is delicious and easy to make. The secret to these granola bars is dates, which give them a naturally sweet flavor and a pleasantly sticky texture and make them refined sugar-free.

PER SERVING

CALORIES:
324

TOTAL FAT:
13 G

CARBS:
43 G

FIBER:
7 G

PROTEIN:
10 G

CALCIUM:
46 MG

VITAMIN D:
0 MCG

VITAMIN B12:
0 MCG

IRON:
3 MG

ZINC:
1 MG

1½ cups rolled oats
2½ cups pitted Medjool dates
½ cup toasted pumpkin seeds
½ cup sunflower seeds
2 teaspoons ground flaxseed
1 heaping teaspoon Dutch process
   cocoa powder (optional)

1 teaspoon ground cinnamon
1 teaspoon vanilla extract
¼ teaspoon salt
¼ cup all-natural peanut butter

1. Preheat the oven to 350°F. Line an 8-inch square baking dish with parchment paper (leaving some hanging over the edges). Spread the rolled oats out in a single layer. Bake for 10 minutes until the oats are lightly golden. Set aside to cool.

2. Add the dates to a food processor and pulse until the dates form a ball. Transfer the dates to a large bowl and add the pumpkin seeds, sunflower seeds, ground flaxseed, salt, cocoa powder, if using, cinnamon, vanilla, salt, and toasted oats. Using your hands, mix until well combined.

3. Melt the peanut butter in the microwave until runny. Pour it over the date mixture and mix well to combine. If the mixture is still stiff, add 2 tablespoons of water to thin it slightly.

4. Press firmly into the prepared baking dish, filling out all corners and leveling off the top. Refrigerate for 1 hour to set. Remove from the pan and cut it into bars. Store in the fridge in an airtight container for up to a week.

Oatmeal Muffins with Carrot and Zucchini

MAKES
12 MUFFINS

PREP TIME
10 MINUTES

COOK TIME
20 MINUTES

I almost always have a batch of these muffins ready to eat. They're an easy way to sneak my kids an extra serving of veggies, and they make a great on-the-go breakfast or snack. I like them because they get my kids to eat vegetables they wouldn't normally choose, and my kids like them because they're a sweet treat. If you have a mini muffin tin, try making mini muffins for a bite-size snack!

1 tablespoon ground flaxseed

3 tablespoons hot water

1½ cups all-purpose flour

1 cup rolled oats

¼ cup packed brown sugar

1 tablespoon baking powder

¼ teaspoon salt

¼ teaspoon ground cinnamon

¼ teaspoon ground ginger

¼ teaspoon ground nutmeg

¼ cup unsweetened applesauce

1 cup unsweetened soy milk

1 teaspoon vanilla extract

½ cup peeled and shredded zucchini

½ cup peeled and shredded carrots

1. Preheat the oven to 375°F. Grease or line a standard muffin tin.

2. Make a flaxseed egg by combining the ground flaxseed and hot water in a small bowl. Set aside to thicken for 5 minutes.

3. In a large bowl, combine the flour, rolled oats, brown sugar, baking powder, salt, cinnamon, ginger, and nutmeg.

4. In a smaller bowl, combine the flaxseed egg, applesauce, milk, and vanilla extract. Add the shredded zucchini and carrots. Stir until combined.

5. Pour the wet ingredients into the dry and stir until just combined.

6. Using a 1½-inch ice cream scoop, divide the batter evenly into a prepared muffin tin. Bake for 20 minutes or until a toothpick inserted in the center of each muffin comes out clean. Serve or store in an airtight container.

VARIATION TIP: For added texture and flavor, add half a cup of chopped pecans, almonds, or walnuts to the muffin batter before baking. Or turn them into "morning glory" muffins by swapping out the applesauce for crushed pineapple and adding raisins.

PER SERVING

CALORIES:
116

TOTAL FAT:
1 G

CARBS:
23 G

FIBER:
3 G

PROTEIN:
4 G

CALCIUM:
71 MG

VITAMIN D:
0 MCG

VITAMIN B12:
0 MCG

IRON:
1 MG

ZINC:
0 MG

Cinnamon Oatmeal Hemp Muffins

MAKES
12 MUFFINS

PREP TIME
5 MINUTES

COOK TIME
20 MINUTES

PER SERVING

CALORIES:
182

TOTAL FAT:
9 G

CARBS:
21 G

FIBER:
3 G

PROTEIN:
6 G

CALCIUM:
89 MG

VITAMIN D:
0 MCG

VITAMIN B12:
0 MCG

IRON:
2 MG

ZINC:
1 MG

In recent years, hemp seeds have become quite common in grocery and bulk stores, making them an easy choice for baking and cooking. Hemp seeds, also called hemp hearts, are the edible seed of the hemp plant. They're also a nutritional powerhouse—they contain protein, iron, fiber, vitamins, and calcium and have a nice earthy texture. Try sprinkling them on top of salads or in soups and chili.

1 tablespoon ground flaxseed

3 tablespoons hot water

1½ cups all-purpose flour

½ cup rolled oats

½ cup hemp seeds

1 tablespoon baking powder

½ cup brown sugar

¼ teaspoon salt

2 teaspoons ground cinnamon

1 cup soy milk

¼ cup vegetable oil

1 tablespoon vanilla extract

1. Make a flaxseed egg by combining the flaxseed and hot water in a small bowl. Set aside to thicken for 5 minutes.

2. Preheat the oven to 375°F. Grease or line a standard 12-cup muffin tin.

3. In a large bowl, combine the flour, rolled oats, hemp seeds, baking powder, brown sugar, salt, and cinnamon. Add the flaxseed egg, soy milk, vegetable oil, and vanilla extract. Stir until just incorporated and it forms a thick batter.

4. Using a 1½-inch ice cream scoop, divide the batter evenly into the prepared muffin tray. Bake for 20 minutes or until a toothpick inserted into the center of each muffin comes out clean. Serve or store in an airtight container.

VARIATION TIP: To add a crunchy topping to these muffins, combine 2 tablespoons of granulated sugar with 1 teaspoon of ground cinnamon. Sprinkle the mixture on top of the muffins before baking. Or, try adding chopped pecans to the batter for even more crunch.

Peanut Butter Banana Overnight Oats

SERVES
2

PREP TIME
10 MINUTES
+ CHILL TIME

Overnight oats are a great, nutritious way to eat oatmeal without having to cook it. Cooked oats are healthy, but they do lose some nutritional value when heated. To make overnight oats, you'll need jars with screw-top lids. I prefer to use wide-mouth 8-ounce mason jars, which you can find in the canning section of most grocery or home goods stores. If you don't have mason jars, an old pasta sauce or pickle jar works, too.

1 cup rolled oats

2 teaspoons chia seeds

1 cup unsweetened almond milk

2 teaspoons maple syrup

1 teaspoon vanilla extract

½ teaspoon ground cinnamon

2 tablespoons creamy
  peanut butter

1 large banana, sliced

1. Add the rolled oats and chia seeds to the bottom of a mason jar. Cover with the almond milk, maple syrup, vanilla extract, and cinnamon. Top with the peanut butter and sliced banana.

2. Seal the jar and chill for at least two hours (or overnight). When ready, stir the contents of the jar and serve.

VARIATION TIP: The base recipe here is oats, chia seeds, plant-based milk (or yogurt), and a sweetener, like maple syrup. Once you've got that, you can get really creative with flavors and additions, like piña colada (coconut and pineapple), mixed berries, PB and J, and even French toast (½ teaspoon cinnamon and ¼ teaspoon each nutmeg and ginger).

PER SERVING

CALORIES:
365

TOTAL FAT:
13 G

CARBS:
52 G

FIBER:
9 G

PROTEIN:
11 G

CALCIUM:
308 MG

VITAMIN D:
50 MCG

VITAMIN B12:
0 MCG

IRON:
3 MG

ZINC:
2 MG

Strawberry Chia Overnight Oats

SERVES
2

PREP TIME
10 MINUTES
+ CHILL TIME

PER SERVING

CALORIES:
345

TOTAL FAT:
6 G

CARBS:
65 G

FIBER:
9 G

PROTEIN:
7 G

CALCIUM:
520 MG

VITAMIN D:
50 MCG

VITAMIN B12:
0 MCG

IRON:
7 MG

ZINC:
2 MG

Add extra flavor and creaminess to your overnight oats by incorporating vegan yogurt. For this recipe, I recommend using Daiya strawberry yogurt, though if you can't find it, any other brand of vegan strawberry yogurt will do. If flavored yogurts aren't available at your grocery store, use a vanilla or plain vegan yogurt and mix in 1 to 2 tablespoons of strawberry jam.

1 cup vegan strawberry yogurt

3 tablespoons maple syrup

1 teaspoon vanilla extract

1 cup unsweetened almond milk

1 cup rolled oats

2 teaspoons chia seeds

¼ teaspoon salt

1 cup fresh strawberries, sliced, for topping

2 tablespoons almond butter, for topping (optional)

1. In a large bowl, combine the yogurt, maple syrup, vanilla extract, and almond milk. Stir until just combined. Add the oats, chia seeds, and salt. Stir until combined.

2. Pour into mason jars. Seal and refrigerate for a minimum of two hours or up to overnight.

3. Top with the fresh strawberries and almond butter, if using. Stir before serving.

TECHNIQUE TIP: If the oats are too thick after sitting overnight, add almond milk 1 tablespoon at a time and stir to thin it.

Rum Raisin Steel-Cut Oatmeal

SERVES
4

PREP TIME
5 MINUTES

COOK TIME
35 MINUTES

Many of us grew up eating steel-cut oats on cold winter days—for me, it's total comfort food. This "rum raisin" version doesn't actually use rum, but it mimics the flavor with maple syrup, butter, vanilla, and, of course, raisins. If you're not a fan of raisins, swap them out for chopped pecans, which also pair beautifully with maple syrup.

3 cups water

2 cups unsweetened almond milk

1 tablespoon vegan butter

¼ teaspoon salt

1½ cups steel-cut oats

½ cup raisins

4 tablespoons maple syrup, plus extra, for drizzling

1 teaspoon ground cinnamon

1 teaspoon vanilla extract

1. In a large saucepan, combine the water, almond milk, butter, and salt, and bring to a boil.

2. Stir in the oats and raisins and return to a boil, then immediately reduce the heat to low. Cover and simmer for 25 minutes, stirring frequently to keep the oats from sticking to the bottom of the pan. The oats should be soft, and the liquid should be mostly evaporated.

3. Remove from the heat and stir in 2 tablespoons of maple syrup, the cinnamon, and the vanilla extract. Cover and let sit for 10 minutes. Stir and serve in bowls with the remaining 2 tablespoons of maple syrup on top.

PREP TIP: Steel-cut oats now come in quick-cook varieties. If you can find them at your local supermarket, use them instead to turn this recipe into a 5-minute weekday morning breakfast.

PER SERVING

CALORIES:
378

TOTAL FAT:
8 G

CARBS:
69 G

FIBER:
7 G

PROTEIN:
9 G

CALCIUM:
304 MG

VITAMIN D:
50 MCG

VITAMIN B12:
0 MCG

IRON:
3 MG

ZINC:
0 MG

Bulgur Biryani

SERVES
4

PREP TIME
15 MINUTES

COOK TIME
30 MINUTES

Biryani is a mixed rice dish from India. It's traditionally made with rice, but this recipe uses bulgur, another delicious grain from the Middle East jam-packed with fiber. To save time in this recipe, the bulgur cooks separately from the vegetables and is added in at the end, making this an easy weeknight dinner.

PER SERVING

CALORIES:
319

TOTAL FAT:
8 G

CARBS:
54 G

FIBER:
15 G

PROTEIN:
10 G

CALCIUM:
112 MG

VITAMIN D:
0 MCG

VITAMIN B12:
0 MCG

IRON:
3 MG

ZINC:
1 MG

2 teaspoons Basic Curry Paste (page 20) or 2 tablespoons curry powder
1⅓ cups vegetable broth
⅔ cup wheat bulgur
2 tablespoons extra-virgin olive oil
1 medium onion, diced
½ green bell pepper, diced
½ red bell pepper, diced
1 garlic clove, minced
1 tablespoon grated ginger

1 (15-ounce) can diced tomatoes, drained
½ cup water
1½ cups frozen mixed vegetables (peas, carrots, green beans)
1 teaspoon ground cumin
½ teaspoon ground turmeric
½ teaspoon ground black pepper
½ teaspoon salt
½ teaspoon ground cinnamon
½ teaspoon sriracha

1. Prepare the Basic Curry Paste, if using.

2. In a medium-size pot with a tight-fitting lid, bring the vegetable broth to a boil. Stir in the bulgur. Cover and reduce the heat to medium-low. Cook for 12 minutes. Remove from heat and let stand, covered, for 10 minutes.

3. In a large pan with a tight-fitting lid, heat the oil over medium-high heat. Add the onion and cook for 3 to 4 minutes or until translucent. Add the bell peppers, garlic, ginger, tomatoes, and water. Cook until the water is mostly evaporated, about 5 minutes.

4. Add the frozen mixed vegetables, curry paste, cumin, turmeric, black pepper, salt, cinnamon, and sriracha. Cook until the vegetables are warmed through. Add the cooked bulgur and stir to combine. Serve immediately.

VARIATION TIP: Try pairing this dish with Chana Masala (page 79). To cool it down a bit, serve some White Garlic Dill Sauce (page 27) on the side.

Roasted Root Vegetable Barley Bowl

SERVES
3 TO 4

PREP TIME
15 MINUTES

COOK TIME
30 MINUTES

Bowls are a great way to enjoy a wide variety of vegetables, grains, and proteins in a compact dish. For this recipe, I recommend using pearl barley, which is available at most bulk food and grocery stores. Pearl barley has had its tough outer hulls removed, making it faster to cook. If using hulled barley, add another 15 to 20 minutes for cooking.

3 cups vegetable broth
1 cup pearl barley
2 medium sweet potatoes, cubed
2 carrots, chopped
2 parsnips, chopped
½ butternut squash, cubed
5 tablespoons extra-virgin olive oil, divided

1 teaspoon salt
1 teaspoon ground black pepper
1 medium onion, diced
2 garlic cloves, diced
4 cups fresh baby spinach leaves
¼ cup water
1 cup Lemon Tahini Vinaigrette (page 34)

PER SERVING

CALORIES:
656

TOTAL FAT:
46 G

CARBS:
59 G

FIBER:
15 G

PROTEIN:
12 G

CALCIUM:
276 MG

VITAMIN D:
0 MCG

VITAMIN B12:
1 MCG

IRON:
5 MG

ZINC:
3 MG

1. Preheat the oven to 400°F. Line a standard baking sheet with parchment paper.

2. In a large saucepan with a tight-fitting lid, bring the vegetable broth to a boil. Add the barley and stir. Reduce the heat to low, cover, and simmer for 25 minutes or until the barley is tender and the liquid is absorbed. Set aside to cool.

3. Spread the sweet potatoes, carrots, parsnips, and butternut squash in an even layer on the baking sheet. Drizzle with 3 tablespoons of olive oil, salt, and pepper. Toss to coat. Bake for 20 to 25 minutes or until the vegetables are caramelized.

4. While the barley and vegetables cook, heat the remaining 2 tablespoons of olive oil over medium-high heat in a wide skillet. Add the onion and cook until translucent, about 5 minutes. Add the garlic and cook for 1 minute.

5. Add the spinach and water to the skillet. Cover and steam for 3 minutes. Remove the lid and continue cooking, stirring constantly, until the spinach wilts. Remove from heat.

CONTINUED >

6. While the vegetables finish cooking, prepare the Lemon Tahini Vinaigrette.

7. Remove the vegetables from the oven.

8. Construct the bowls by placing ½ cup of barley on the bottom. Layer with the roasted vegetables and sautéed spinach and onions. Drizzle with the vinaigrette.

PREP TIP: Barley is a great grain (and a great rice substitute) to keep on hand for a variety of dishes. Try making a batch (or two) on the weekend and store it in the fridge for use throughout the week to reduce cooking time for weeknight meals.

Mom's Tomato Rice

SERVES
4

PREP TIME
10 MINUTES

COOK TIME
20 MINUTES

Growing up, my mom had this spiced tomato-rice dish that she called "Spanish Rice." It wasn't like Spanish (or Mexican) rice that you'd get from a restaurant, and it wasn't Spanish rice like you'd find in paella. It got its name from an old cookbook. Whatever the origin, I loved it growing up, and I think about it often. My mother's version wasn't vegan, but I've come up with a pretty close vegan replica.

1 cup Meaty Tofu Crumble
   (page 17)
2 cups basmati rice
4 cups vegetable broth
⅓ cup tomato sauce
1 teaspoon dried oregano
1 teaspoon dried basil
1 teaspoon dried thyme

½ teaspoon salt
½ teaspoon ground black pepper
2 tablespoons extra-virgin olive oil
1 medium onion, diced
1 green bell pepper, diced
1 (15-ounce) can small kidney
   beans, drained and rinsed

PER SERVING

CALORIES:
376

TOTAL FAT:
12 G

CARBS:
53 G

FIBER:
9 G

PROTEIN:
16 G

CALCIUM:
180 MG

VITAMIN D:
0 MCG

VITAMIN B12:
0 MCG

IRON:
4 MG

ZINC:
1 MG

1. Prepare the Meaty Tofu Crumble.

2. In a medium pot with a tight-fitting lid, combine the basmati rice, vegetable broth, tomato sauce, oregano, basil, thyme, salt, and pepper. Stir well. Bring to a boil, then reduce heat to low, cover, and cook for 18 to 20 minutes or until the rice is tender and the liquid is absorbed. Set aside when done.

3. In a large, deep skillet, heat the oil over medium-high heat. Add the onion and bell pepper and cook until the onion is translucent and the bell pepper is soft.

4. Add the tofu crumble and stir until warmed through.

5. Add the cooked rice and kidney beans to the pan and stir to combine.

STRETCH TIP: If you have leftovers, this rice makes a great filling for burritos or enchiladas or even in a bowl. Try using it in place of barley in the Barley Burrito Bowl (page 147).

Roasted Rainbow Veg with Pearl Couscous

SERVES
4

PREP TIME
20 MINUTES

COOK TIME
20 MINUTES

PER SERVING

CALORIES:
636

TOTAL FAT:
29 G

CARBS:
72 G

FIBER:
5 G

PROTEIN:
29 G

CALCIUM:
189 MG

VITAMIN D:
0 MCG

VITAMIN B12:
0 MCG

IRON:
6 MG

ZINC:
2 MG

This is a great family-style dish—it's served on a large platter so everyone can help themselves (and there's no pesky plating). I like to use pearl couscous for this dish because it's larger and more substantial than regular couscous, which is quite small and grainy. Pearl couscous (also known as Israeli couscous) is available at most grocery and bulk food stores.

2½ cups vegetable broth
2 cups pearl couscous
1 red bell pepper, diced
1 yellow bell pepper, diced
1 large carrot, grated
1 red onion, diced
2 cups asparagus, chopped
2 cups grape tomatoes, halved
  lengthwise

1 block extra-firm tofu, cubed
2 tablespoons extra-virgin olive oil
½ teaspoon salt
½ teaspoon ground black pepper
3 tablespoons lime juice
1 tablespoon maple syrup
½ teaspoon chili powder

1. Preheat the oven to 400°F. Line a large rimmed baking sheet with parchment paper.

2. Make the couscous. In a medium-size pot, bring the vegetable broth to a boil. Stir in the couscous and reduce the heat to low. Cover and simmer for 10 minutes, or until the liquid is absorbed. Fluff the couscous with a fork and set aside.

3. Spread the bell peppers, carrot, onion, asparagus, tomatoes, and tofu on the baking sheet in a single layer. Drizzle with the olive oil, salt, and pepper. Roast for 15 to 20 minutes or until the vegetables are soft and caramelized.

4. In a small bowl, make the dressing by whisking together the lime juice, maple syrup, and chili powder.

5. Transfer the couscous to a long serving platter and spread it out to form an even layer. Top with roasted vegetables and drizzle with dressing.

VARIATION TIP: Instead of serving on a platter, stuff the couscous and vegetables into pita pockets with lettuce and drizzle with Lemon Tahini Vinaigrette (page 34). Or, skip the pita and serve it in a bowl on top of leafy greens.

Barley Burrito Bowl

SERVES
4

PREP TIME
10 MINUTES

COOK TIME
25 MINUTES

These quick and easy Barley Burrito Bowls combine the delicious flavors and textures of black and kidney beans, salsa, avocado, chili powder, lime, and, of course, nutrient-packed barley. If you want even more texture in this dish, crush some corn tortilla chips on top for some added crunch.

3 cups vegetable broth

1 cup pearl barley

1 cup Pico de Gallo (page 23) or store-bought salsa

½ cup Vegan Caesar Dressing (page 34)

1 cup canned black beans, drained and rinsed

1 cup canned kidney beans, drained and rinsed

1 (7-ounce) can corn kernels

3 tablespoons lime juice

1 tablespoon maple syrup

½ teaspoon chili powder

½ teaspoon salt

½ teaspoon ground black pepper

½ head iceberg lettuce, shredded

2 avocados, cubed

PER SERVING

CALORIES:
586

TOTAL FAT:
31 G

CARBS:
119 G

FIBER:
34 G

PROTEIN:
30 G

CALCIUM:
235 MG

VITAMIN D:
4 MCG

VITAMIN B12:
1 MCG

IRON:
7 MG

ZINC:
5 MG

1. In a large saucepan with a tight-fitting lid, bring the vegetable broth to a boil. Add the barley, stirring to combine. Reduce heat to low, cover, and simmer for 25 minutes, or until the barley is tender and the liquid is absorbed. Set aside to cool.

2. While the barley is cooking, prepare the Pico de Gallo and Vegan Caesar Dressing.

3. Make the bean mixture. In a medium bowl, combine the black beans, kidney beans, corn, and pico de gallo. Set aside.

4. Make the lettuce mixture. In a small bowl, whisk together the lime juice, maple syrup, chili powder, salt, and pepper. Toss with the lettuce to coat.

5. Divide the lettuce evenly between four wide serving bowls. Top with ¼ to ½ cup cooked barley, the bean mixture, and avocado. Drizzle with the Caesar dressing.

STRETCH TIP: Use up any leftover tortillas from taco night to turn this bowl into a burrito. Simply layer all ingredients down the middle of a large tortilla, fold in the sides, then fold up from the bottom, tucking in as you go. Grill each side for 3 minutes on medium-high heat, or eat as is.

Kitchen Sink Buckwheat Ramen

SERVES
4 TO 6

PREP TIME
15 MINUTES

COOK TIME
15 MINUTES

PER SERVING

CALORIES:
983

TOTAL FAT:
22 G

CARBS:
88 G

FIBER:
23 G

PROTEIN:
18 G

CALCIUM:
150 MG

VITAMIN D:
2 MCG

VITAMIN B12:
1 MCG

IRON:
5 MG

ZINC:
3 MG

Buckwheat noodles, or soba noodles, are a staple of Japanese cooking, used in numerous soups and hot or cold noodle dishes. Pure, 100 percent buckwheat noodles are gluten-free, so although not typical, I often use them to make vegan "ramen" for my gluten-intolerant husband. As with many soups, this recipe is a great starting point: You can follow the exact recipe or customize your bowl with veggies you have on hand.

¼ cup Stir-Fry Sauce (page 28), divided

1 (14-ounce) package soba or buckwheat noodles

2 tablespoons extra-virgin olive oil

½ medium onion, diced

3 garlic cloves, minced

1 tablespoon fresh ginger, grated

¼ teaspoon red pepper flakes

¼ teaspoon ground cinnamon

2 tablespoons water

1 red bell pepper, thinly sliced into strips

1 block firm tofu, cubed

8 cups vegetable broth

3 tablespoons soy sauce

2 cups baby bok choy, chopped

1 cup frozen or canned corn

1 avocado, cubed, for garnish

3 scallions, finely chopped, for garnish

1. Prepare the Stir-Fry Sauce.

2. Make the noodles. Boil a large pot of water. Add the soba noodles and cook according to package directions (usually 5 to 7 minutes). While cooking, fill a large bowl with cold tap water. Set aside.

3. Drain the cooked noodles in a colander and immediately submerge them in the bowl of cold water. Keep submerged for 2 minutes to halt the cooking process. Drain again in the colander and set aside.

4. Make the soup. In a large pot, heat the olive oil over medium-high heat. Add the onion and cook until translucent, about 5 minutes. Add the garlic, ginger, red pepper flakes, cinnamon, and water. Cook for 2 minutes or until fragrant. Add the bell pepper and tofu, and cook for 5 minutes.

5. Add the vegetable broth, 2 tablespoons of Stir-Fry Sauce, the soy sauce, and the bok choy. Bring to a boil, then simmer for 5 minutes. Add the corn and stir until warmed through.

6. Divide the noodles between 4 large soup bowls. Ladle the soup over the noodles and top with the avocado, scallions, and remaining Stir-Fry Sauce.

TECHNIQUE TIP: Buckwheat noodles can be finicky, so be sure to follow the cooking time indicated on the package. Shocking the noodles in cold water keeps them from sticking together and getting mushy.

Broccoli Cheddar Rice

SERVES
3 TO 4

PREP TIME
10 MINUTES

COOK TIME
20 MINUTES

PER SERVING

CALORIES:
758

TOTAL FAT:
25 G

CARBS:
109 G

FIBER:
6 G

PROTEIN:
24 G

CALCIUM:
345 MG

VITAMIN D:
0 MCG

VITAMIN B12:
0 MCG

IRON:
4 MG

ZINC:
1 MG

One of my favorite things to do in the kitchen is to turn side dishes into actual meals. Growing up, rice was always served as a side dish, and it wasn't until I moved out on my own that I realized it could be a main dish if I wanted it to be. Broccoli and Cheddar is a classic flavor combination, and it helps the rice stand on its own.

4 cups vegetable broth

2 cups basmati rice

1 cup Smoky Tofu "Bacon," crumbled (page 18)

1 head broccoli, cut into florets

3 tablespoons water

3 tablespoons vegan butter

3 tablespoons all-purpose flour

3 cups unsweetened soy milk

1 teaspoon ground mustard

½ teaspoon dried thyme

¼ teaspoon ground nutmeg

½ teaspoon salt

½ teaspoon ground black pepper

2 teaspoons nutritional yeast

1½ cups vegan Cheddar-style shreds

1. In a medium pot, bring the vegetable broth to a boil. Add the rice and reduce heat to low. Cover and cook for 15 to 18 minutes or until the rice is cooked through and the liquid is absorbed. Remove from heat.

2. While the rice cooks, prepare the crumbled Smoky Tofu "Bacon."

3. Steam the broccoli by placing the florets into a microwave-safe bowl. Add 3 tablespoons of water. Cover with a microwave-safe plate and microwave on high for 2 to 4 minutes or until the broccoli is tender. Set aside.

4. Make the Cheddar sauce. In a large pot, melt the butter over medium-high heat. Add the flour and stir constantly until it forms a thick paste. Pour in the soy milk in a slow, steady stream and whisk constantly until no lumps remain.

5. Add the ground mustard, thyme, nutmeg, salt, pepper, and nutritional yeast. Simmer for 8 to 10 minutes or until the sauce thickens. Add the vegan Cheddar-style shreds and whisk until melted.

6. Add the rice and broccoli to the cheese sauce and stir to combine. Transfer to a 9-by-13-inch serving dish and top with the crumbled tofu "bacon."

Roasted Sweet Potato and Spinach Quinoa Bowl

SERVES
4

PREP TIME
10 MINUTES

COOK TIME
25 MINUTES

This bowl makes a delicious, protein-packed lunch or dinner. I like to make a large batch of quinoa at the beginning of the week so I always have it ready to go for quick and easy meals. For extra flavor, cook the quinoa in vegetable broth instead of water.

4 cups cooked quinoa (or 1 cup dry quinoa)

3 large sweet potatoes, cubed

4 tablespoons extra-virgin olive oil, divided

½ teaspoon salt

1 teaspoon ground black pepper

½ teaspoon ground cinnamon

1 cup Lemon Tahini Vinaigrette (page 34)

½ medium onion, diced

1 garlic clove, minced

¼ teaspoon ground nutmeg

4 cups fresh baby spinach leaves

¼ cup water, reserved from the quinoa

1 to 2 avocados, cubed

PER SERVING

CALORIES:
857

TOTAL FAT:
51 G

CARBS:
88 G

FIBER:
16 G

PROTEIN:
18 G

CALCIUM:
225 MG

VITAMIN D:
0 MCG

VITAMIN B12:
1 MCG

IRON:
7 MG

ZINC:
4 MG

1. Cook the quinoa according to package directions, if necessary, reserving ¼ cup of water. Set aside.

2. To make the sweet potatoes, preheat the oven to 400°F. Line a large baking sheet with parchment paper. Spread the sweet potatoes evenly on the baking sheet and drizzle with 2 tablespoons of olive oil, salt, pepper, and cinnamon. Toss to coat. Bake for 15 to 20 minutes or until the sweet potatoes are tender and golden. While the potatoes cook, prepare the Lemon Tahini Vinaigrette.

3. In a deep skillet, heat the remaining 2 tablespoons of olive oil over medium-high heat. Add the onion and cook until translucent, about 5 minutes. Add the garlic and nutmeg to the skillet and cook for 1 minute.

4. Add the spinach and reserved water to the skillet. Cover and steam for 5 minutes. Remove the lid and stir until the spinach is wilted, about 3 minutes.

5. Divide the quinoa between 4 serving bowls. Top with the sweet potatoes, spinach, and avocado. Drizzle with Lemon Tahini Vinaigrette.

Ginger Tofu with Rice Noodles

SERVES
4

PREP TIME
5 MINUTES

COOK TIME
10 MINUTES

PER SERVING

CALORIES:
271

TOTAL FAT:
15 G

CARBS:
25 G

FIBER:
2 G

PROTEIN:
11 G

CALCIUM:
280 MG

VITAMIN D:
0 MCG

VITAMIN B12:
0 MCG

IRON:
3 MG

ZINC:
2 MG

This is one of my go-to weeknight dinners. It comes together in 15 minutes, so you can put a hearty, warm dinner on the table no matter how hectic your day. The surprise ingredient in this dish is tahini. It's wonderfully creamy and nutty and makes a lovely base for the sauce.

1 (10-ounce) package broad rice noodles

1 (12-ounce) block extra-firm tofu, cubed

1 tablespoon cornstarch

2 tablespoons extra-virgin olive oil

2 tablespoons tahini

2 teaspoons soy sauce

2 teaspoons maple syrup

1½ teaspoons grated fresh ginger

½ teaspoon sriracha

½ lime, juiced

1. Cook the noodles according to package directions. Set aside.

2. In a medium bowl, toss the tofu with the cornstarch to coat. In a deep skillet, heat the olive oil over medium-high heat. Add the tofu and fry on all sides until crispy and golden, about 10 minutes.

3. In a small bowl, combine the tahini, soy sauce, maple syrup, ginger, sriracha, and lime juice. Whisk well to combine. Pour over the tofu in the pan.

4. Add the rice noodles and toss to combine.

VARIATION TIP: This dish is a great canvas for all kinds of leftover vegetables, so raid your fridge and see what you have hanging around. Slice or dice bell peppers, carrots, celery, bok choy, or steamed broccoli, or grab a cup of frozen peas or corn and toss them in.

Golden Curry Veggies and Rice

This dish is bright and colorful in both appearance and flavor. The warm heat from the curry combined with rich coconut milk provides a canvas for a wide variety of vegetables. I typically serve this curry on rice, but if you have them around, you could use potatoes instead, cooking them in the pot with the cauliflower and carrots. To add a cool, crunchy element, try serving this curry with diced cucumbers and a dollop of White Garlic Dill Sauce (page 27).

SERVES
4

PREP TIME
10 MINUTES

COOK TIME
30 MINUTES

PER SERVING

CALORIES:
538

TOTAL FAT:
10 G

CARBS:
97 G

FIBER:
6 G

PROTEIN:
13 G

CALCIUM:
134 MG

VITAMIN D:
50 MCG

VITAMIN B12:
1 MCG

IRON:
1 MG

ZINC:
1 MG

2 to 3 tablespoons Basic Curry Paste (page 20)
5 cups vegetable broth, divided
2 cups basmati rice
1 head cauliflower, cut into florets
2 large carrots, chopped
2 tablespoons extra-virgin olive oil
1 large onion, diced

2 garlic cloves, minced
1 teaspoon grated ginger
1 (15-ounce) can diced tomatoes, drained
1 (14-ounce) can coconut milk
1 cup frozen peas
Cooked rice, for serving

1. Prepare the Basic Curry Paste.

2. In a medium pot, bring 4 cups of vegetable broth to a boil. Pour in the rice, reduce heat to low, and simmer, covered, for 15 to 18 minutes or until the rice is cooked and the liquid is absorbed. Set aside.

3. Bring a large pot of water to a boil. Add the cauliflower and carrots, and cook until fork-tender, about 10 minutes. Drain and set aside.

4. In a deep skillet, heat the olive oil on medium-high heat. Add the onion and cook until translucent, about 5 minutes. Add the garlic, ginger, curry paste, and diced tomatoes, and cook until fragrant, about 2 minutes, stirring constantly.

5. Pour in the coconut milk and the remaining 1 cup of vegetable broth. Simmer until the sauce thickens, about 10 minutes.

6. Add the cooked cauliflower and carrots and the frozen peas. Stir for 1 minute to combine. The residual heat from the dish will warm the peas quickly. Serve over rice.

Cheddar Jalapeño Corn Bread, 161

7

Snacks and Sides

Rosemary and Dill "Smashed" Potatoes

SERVES
4

PREP TIME
5 MINUTES

COOK TIME
35 MINUTES

PER SERVING

CALORIES:
241

TOTAL FAT:
14 G

CARBS:
26 G

FIBER:
3 G

PROTEIN:
3 G

CALCIUM:
25 MG

VITAMIN D:
0 MCG

VITAMIN B12:
0 MCG

IRON:
2 MG

ZINC:
0 MG

This is a fantastic but effortless side dish with a real "wow" factor. It doesn't require much time because it can cook alongside whatever main dish you're making. As a shortcut, I start by microwaving the potatoes most of the way before finishing them off in the oven. I find this dish works best with yellow potatoes (sometimes called Yukon gold potatoes) because of their hearty composition.

4 large yellow potatoes, skins on, scrubbed

4 tablespoons extra-virgin olive oil

½ teaspoon salt

½ teaspoon ground black pepper

1 teaspoon dried dill

1 teaspoon dried rosemary

1. Preheat the oven to 425°F. Line a large baking sheet with parchment paper.

2. Using a fork or a paring knife, poke holes around the entire surface of each potato (this will keep it from exploding in the microwave). Place the potatoes on a microwave-safe plate and cook on high for 12 to 15 minutes, or until tender all the way through.

3. Place the microwaved potatoes on a prepared baking sheet, spread evenly apart. Grab a small plate and place it on top of one potato. Using your palms, press down firmly on the plate to flatten or "smash" the potato to ¾- to 1-inch thickness. Repeat with the remaining potatoes.

4. Drizzle the olive oil evenly over all four smashed potatoes, then sprinkle salt, pepper, dill, and rosemary over them. Bake for 15 to 20 minutes, or until the edges are crispy and golden. Serve immediately.

TECHNIQUE TIP: If you have fresh rosemary, you can use it in place of dried—but use a little less, as fresh rosemary is quite aromatic and can overpower a dish. That being said, your kitchen will smell lovely as it cooks.

Maple Pecan Sautéed Brussels Sprouts

SERVES
4 TO 6

PREP TIME
10 MINUTES

COOK TIME
5 TO 10 MINUTES

These sautéed Brussels sprouts are just as delicious as the slow-roasted kind you might find at a fancy restaurant or on your mom's Thanksgiving table—but they're quick enough to make on busy weeknights. Shredding the sprouts drastically reduces their cooking time, so you'll need to use a food processor or a grater to shred them. Alternatively, buy pre-shredded sprouts at the grocery store.

1½ pounds whole Brussels sprouts
2 tablespoons extra-virgin olive oil
1 tablespoon vegan butter
1 teaspoon salt

1 teaspoon ground black pepper
½ cup pecan halves
2 tablespoons maple syrup

PER SERVING

CALORIES:
178

TOTAL FAT:
12 G

CARBS:
16 G

FIBER:
5 G

PROTEIN:
5 G

CALCIUM:
62 MG

VITAMIN D:
0 MCG

VITAMIN B12:
0 MCG

IRON:
2 MG

ZINC:
1 MG

1. If necessary, grate the Brussels sprouts or shred them in a food processor fitted with the large slicing disc if they are whole.

2. In a large skillet, heat the olive oil over medium-high heat. Add the shredded Brussels sprouts and toss to coat. Cook for about 4 minutes.

3. Add the butter, salt, pepper, and pecan halves. Cook, stirring constantly, for about 2 minutes, then add the maple syrup. Stir to coat and cook for 1 minute. Serve immediately.

VARIATION TIP: To give this dish a holiday feel, swap the pecans and maple syrup for balsamic vinegar, red pepper flakes, and Smoky Tofu "Bacon" (page 18). Follow the recipe, adding the tofu "bacon" at the very end so that it warms through but doesn't overcook.

Quick Green Bean Casserole

SERVES
4

PREP TIME
10 MINUTES

COOK TIME
20 MINUTES

PER SERVING

CALORIES:
373

TOTAL FAT:
22 G

CARBS:
39 G

FIBER:
9 G

PROTEIN:
9 G

CALCIUM:
186 MG

VITAMIN D:
19 MCG

VITAMIN B12:
0 MCG

IRON:
5 MG

ZINC:
1 MG

I like to think of this as a deconstructed green bean casserole. In this recipe, we're skipping the baked-in-the-oven part, using a skillet instead to save time without skimping on flavor. For an added twist, I've switched out half the green beans, opting for a combination of green and yellow wax beans. The red pepper flakes add a bit of warmth to the dish, but they're totally optional—if heat isn't your thing, skip them.

½ pound green beans, trimmed and halved

½ pound yellow wax beans, trimmed and halved

2 tablespoons extra-virgin olive oil

½ red onion, diced

2 ounces cremini mushrooms, stemmed and caps thinly sliced

½ teaspoon salt

½ teaspoon ground black pepper

¼ teaspoon red pepper flakes

2 tablespoons all-purpose flour

1 cup vegetable broth

¾ cup unsweetened almond milk

2 teaspoons nutritional yeast

½ teaspoon ground mustard

¼ teaspoon ground nutmeg

2 cups store-bought crispy fried onions, such as French's

1. Bring a large pot of water to a boil. Add the beans and cook for 5 minutes, until tender. Drain and run the beans under cold water for 1 minute to stop the cooking process. Set aside.

2. Heat the olive oil in a wide skillet over medium-high heat. Add the onion, mushrooms, salt, pepper, and red pepper flakes, and cook for about 5 minutes, or until the mushrooms soften and the onion is translucent.

3. Add the flour and toss until the onions and mushrooms are coated. Pour in the vegetable broth and milk and whisk to combine. Add the nutritional yeast, mustard, and nutmeg. Bring to a boil, then reduce the heat to medium and simmer until it becomes a thick soup, 8 to 10 minutes.

4. Remove from the heat and add the green and yellow beans and crispy fried onions. Toss well to coat. Serve immediately.

Red Potato Salad

SERVES
4

PREP TIME
25 MINUTES

COOK TIME
7 MINUTES

I love bringing this dish to potlucks and BBQs. Since this recipe doesn't contain mayonnaise, it travels well, and it's a refreshing change from typical potato salad. I use red potatoes in this recipe for their color and because they stand up well to the cooking process. While potato salad is typically served cold, I enjoy serving this one slightly warm—the residual heat from the potatoes warms up the dressing and enhances its flavor.

15 red potatoes, skins on, cut into 1-inch cubes

½ cup extra-virgin olive oil

2 tablespoons lemon juice

2 garlic cloves, minced

2 teaspoons Dijon mustard

¼ cup fresh chopped parsley

1 teaspoon dried dill

1 teaspoon nutritional yeast

1 teaspoon salt

½ teaspoon ground black pepper

PER SERVING

CALORIES:
808

TOTAL FAT:
28 G

CARBS:
129 G

FIBER:
14 G

PROTEIN:
16 G

CALCIUM:
92 MG

VITAMIN D:
0 MCG

VITAMIN B12:
0 MCG

IRON:
6 MG

ZINC:
3 MG

1. To cook the potatoes, add them to a large pot and fill with just enough water to cover. Bring to a boil and cook the potatoes for 5 to 7 minutes, until fork-tender. Drain and set aside to cool almost completely, about 20 minutes.

2. Make the dressing. In a small bowl, whisk together the olive oil, lemon juice, garlic, mustard, parsley, dill, nutritional yeast, salt, and pepper.

3. Transfer the potatoes to a large serving bowl and add the dressing. Toss gently to coat the potatoes. Serve or refrigerate.

PREP TIP: This is a great make-ahead side—you can refrigerate it for up to 3 days before serving, and as it sits, the flavors blend together. Serve this potato salad cold or warm it up gently by placing it in a glass bowl set over a pot with 2 inches of simmering water. Stir occasionally, for 5 to 7 minutes, until warmed through.

Creamy Coleslaw

SERVES
4 TO 6

PREP TIME
5 MINUTES

This is a super-fast side dish—five minutes and you're done. The secret in this recipe is the kick from the yellow mustard. It's fantastic on its own and even better when paired with a good BBQ dish, like my BBQ Tempeh and Caramelized Onion Tavern Burgers (page 59), Crispy Buffalo Tofu Wrap (page 48), or BBQ Pulled Jackfruit Sandwiches (page 109). If you can't find pre-shredded coleslaw mix, shred ½ head each green and purple cabbage and 2 to 3 carrots.

PER SERVING

CALORIES:
305

TOTAL FAT:
28 G

CARBS:
14 G

FIBER:
2 G

PROTEIN:
1 G

CALCIUM:
35 MG

VITAMIN D:
0 MCG

VITAMIN B12:
0 MCG

IRON:
1 MG

ZINC:
0 MG

1 cup Easy 4-Ingredient Vegan
　Mayonnaise (page 21)
1 teaspoon yellow mustard
1 tablespoon white vinegar
1 tablespoon lemon juice

2 tablespoons granulated sugar
1 teaspoon salt
1 teaspoon ground black pepper
1 (16-ounce) bag shredded
　coleslaw mix

1. Prepare the Easy 4-Ingredient Vegan Mayonnaise.

2. In a large bowl, whisk together the mayonnaise, mustard, vinegar, lemon juice, sugar, salt, and pepper. Add the shredded coleslaw and toss to coat.

VARIATION TIP: Jazz up your coleslaw by adding shaved brussels sprouts to this recipe, or swap the coleslaw mix for shredded broccoli slaw mix and add diced apples, dried cranberries, cashews, and Smoky Tofu "Bacon" (page 18).

Cheddar Jalapeño Corn Bread

SERVES
4 TO 6

PREP TIME
5 MINUTES

COOK TIME
25 MINUTES

Corn bread is a fantastic side dish. It's even better loaded up with cheese and jalapeños, or scallions if you don't want as much heat. If you have a cast-iron skillet, try using it to achieve a lovely, slightly crunchy bottom. Preheat a 10-inch cast-iron skillet at 425°F for 10 minutes. Add 2 tablespoons of olive oil and swirl it around to coat the skillet. Pour in the batter and bake for 18 to 20 minutes.

Cooking spray, for greasing
1½ cups all-purpose flour
½ cup yellow cornmeal
2 teaspoons baking powder
½ teaspoon salt

1 cup unsweetened almond milk
3 tablespoons melted vegan butter
1 cup vegan Cheddar-style shreds
2 jalapeños, diced

PER SERVING

CALORIES:
312

TOTAL FAT:
15 G

CARBS:
39 G

FIBER:
4 G

PROTEIN:
5 G

CALCIUM:
197 MG

VITAMIN D:
17 MCG

VITAMIN B12:
0 MCG

IRON:
2 MG

ZINC:
0 MG

1. Preheat the oven to 400°F. Grease a 9-inch square baking dish with cooking spray or vegan butter. Set aside.

2. In a large bowl, whisk the flour, cornmeal, baking powder, and salt. Make a hole in the middle of the bowl, pour in the milk, butter, Cheddar shreds, and jalapeños. Using a fork, bring the dry ingredients up and over the wet ingredients and mix together until just combined.

3. Transfer the batter to the prepared baking dish and bake for 20 minutes, or until a toothpick inserted in the center comes out clean. Cool and serve.

STRETCH TIP: Turn this corn bread batter into a dumpling-style topping for chili. Prepare the chili and transfer it to a 9-by-11-inch baking dish. Drop scoopfuls of corn bread batter on top and bake at 400°F for 20 to 25 minutes, or until the corn bread is fluffy and a toothpick inserted in the center comes out clean.

Garlic Chive Red Mashed Potatoes

SERVES
4 TO 6

PREP TIME
10 MINUTES

COOK TIME
15 MINUTES

PER SERVING

CALORIES:
542

TOTAL FAT:
13 G

CARBS:
96 G

FIBER:
12 G

PROTEIN:
15 G

CALCIUM:
93 MG

VITAMIN D:
1 MCG

VITAMIN B12:
0 MCG

IRON:
5 MG

ZINC:
3 MG

I'm always looking for an excuse to make mashed potatoes. For me, they're the ultimate comfort food, especially when piled high and topped with a generous serving of gravy. Growing up, we always made mashed potatoes with yellow or white spuds, but I've come to love using red potatoes with the skins on. They add a pop of color that looks beautiful with bright green chives. Plus, the skins are the healthiest part of the potato, so why throw them away?

1 cup Mushroom Gravy (page 35)

15 to 18 red potatoes, skins on, cut into 1-inch cubes

¼ cup Garlic and Dill Sunflower Seed Cream Cheese (page 67)

2 tablespoons vegan butter

½ cup unsweetened soy milk

¼ cup fresh chives, diced

1 teaspoon salt

½ teaspoon ground black pepper

1. Prepare the Mushroom Gravy.

2. Place the potatoes in a large pot and add just enough water to cover them. Bring to a boil and cook until the potatoes are soft, about 15 minutes. Drain and return the potatoes to the pot. Mash thoroughly with a potato masher or fork.

3. While the potatoes cook, prepare the Garlic and Dill Sunflower Seed Cream Cheese.

4. Add the vegan butter, milk, cream cheese, chives, salt, and pepper. Stir to combine. Taste and adjust the salt and pepper as needed. Serve with Mushroom Gravy.

PREP TIP: If you need to cook ahead of time, you can keep cooked mashed potatoes warm by placing them in a glass bowl set over a pot with 2 inches of simmering water. The steam from the water will gently warm the potatoes until you're ready to serve them.

Spinach and Bread Casserole

SERVES
4

PREP TIME
10 MINUTES

COOK TIME
35 MINUTES

CALORIES:
237

TOTAL FAT:
15 G

CARBS:
21 G

FIBER:
6 G

PROTEIN:
8 G

CALCIUM:
355 MG

VITAMIN D:
39 MCG

VITAMIN B12:
0 MCG

IRON:
5 MG

ZINC:
2 MG

I'm always looking for new side dishes to bring to holiday dinners or family gatherings. Since most of my extended family are omnivores, I like to prepare dishes that are familiar to them but have a vegan twist. Half the time, they don't even realize that their dish is egg- or dairy-free. This spinach and bread casserole is a great example of a classic side that's easy to veganize.

2 tablespoons extra-virgin olive oil
1 medium onion, diced
2 celery stalks, diced
6 ounces cremini mushrooms, stemmed and caps thinly sliced (about 2 cups)
2 (10-ounce) packages frozen spinach, thawed and squeezed to remove moisture

½ cup water chestnuts, drained and sliced
1 vegetable bouillon cube
2 tablespoons all-purpose flour
1½ cups unsweetened almond milk
2 cups cubed white or whole wheat bread
2 tablespoons vegan butter, melted

1. Preheat the oven to 375°F.

2. In a large skillet, heat the olive oil over medium-high heat. Add the onion, celery, and mushrooms and cook for 5 to 7 minutes, or until the onion is translucent and the celery is soft.

3. Add the spinach, water chestnuts, and vegetable bouillon. Cook and stir until the bouillon is dissolved, about 2 minutes. Add the flour and toss to coat the vegetables.

4. Pour in the milk, stirring constantly. Let it simmer for 8 to 10 minutes over medium heat, or until the sauce has thickened into the consistency of a cream-based soup.

5. Transfer the mixture to a 9-by-13-inch baking dish. Top with the cubed bread and drizzle with the melted butter. Bake for 15 to 20 minutes or until the bread is golden. Serve immediately.

PREP TIP: Prep this dish ahead of time by completing all steps except for baking. Cover the casserole with foil and keep it refrigerated. Bake it at your host's house for 15 to 20 minutes and serve it hot from the oven.

Stuffed Mushroom Caps

Stuffed mushroom caps seem fancy, but truthfully, they're aren't difficult to make. In my pre-vegan teenage years, the Red Lobster crab-stuffed version was a favorite of mine. Once I created my Spicy Tofu "Crab" Salad (page 49), I realized I could veganize those mushroom caps. To save time on this dish, prep the tofu "crab" salad a day or two in advance. Use any extra on a sandwich.

1 cup Spicy Tofu "Crab" Salad (page 49)
1 cup Garlic and Dill Sunflower Seed Cream Cheese (page 67) or 1 (8-ounce) container Daiya plain cream cheese
Cooking spray, for greasing
2 tablespoons extra-virgin olive oil
½ small red onion, finely diced
1 medium celery stalk, finely diced
¼ red bell pepper, finely diced

1 garlic clove, minced
1 tablespoon soy sauce
¼ cup nutritional yeast
⅓ cup panko bread crumbs
1 teaspoon dried oregano
1 teaspoon dried basil
1½ teaspoons dried parsley
2 to 3 dozen large button or cremini mushrooms, stemmed
3 tablespoons vegan butter, melted

1. Prepare the Spicy Tofu "Crab" Salad and Garlic and Dill Sunflower Seed Cream Cheese, if using.

2. Preheat the oven to 400°F. Grease a 15-by-10-inch baking dish with cooking spray or butter.

3. Make the filling. In a large skillet, heat the oil over medium-high heat. Add the onion, celery, bell pepper, garlic, and soy sauce, and cook until the vegetables are soft. Add the nutritional yeast, cream cheese, bread crumbs, oregano, basil, and parsley. Cook, stirring constantly, until the cream cheese is melted, about 3 minutes. Remove from heat and mix in the tofu "crab" salad.

4. Place the mushrooms in a single layer in the baking dish, tops down. Brush with the melted butter. Spoon the filing into each mushroom cap. Bake uncovered for 12 to 15 minutes or until the mushrooms are tender and the topping is golden. Serve immediately.

VARIATION TIP: I also like to stuff these mushrooms with spinach and water chestnuts (instead of tofu "crab"). For a spicier version, try using Tofu Chorizo Crumble (page 16) with vegan mozzarella-style shreds on top.

Quick Pickled Cucumber and Onion Salad

SERVES
4 TO 6

PREP TIME
10 MINUTES
+ CHILL TIME

Growing up, this salad was a Sunday brunch staple, often served with bagels and cream cheese. This salad is fresh yet salty and sweet, and it has always been my favorite salad. To this day, it's a staple in my fridge, and it makes a perfect complement to breakfast. To add a bit of heat to this recipe, dice up a red chili and add it to the marinade or sprinkle in some red pepper flakes.

4 English cucumbers, sliced into thin rounds
1 tablespoon kosher salt
1 medium onion, sliced into half moons

½ cup white vinegar
¼ cup water
1 tablespoon sugar
Pinch ground black pepper

PER SERVING

CALORIES:
46

TOTAL FAT:
0 G

CARBS:
11 G

FIBER:
3 G

PROTEIN:
2 G

CALCIUM:
36 MG

VITAMIN D:
0 MCG

VITAMIN B12:
0 MCG

IRON:
1 MG

ZINC:
0 MG

1. Place the sliced cucumbers in a colander and set the colander inside a large bowl. Sprinkle the cucumbers with the salt and toss to coat. Allow the cucumbers to sit for 30 minutes.

2. Drain and press the cucumbers to remove the remaining water. Transfer them to the large bowl.

3. To make the cucumber marinade, add the onion, vinegar, water, sugar, and pepper to the bowl. Mix well.

4. Cover the bowl or, to save space, transfer the entire mixture to a resealable bag. Refrigerate for 3 to 4 hours before serving.

STRETCH TIP: Keep this salad on hand for quick use when needed. Simply store it in a sealed mason jar in the fridge for up to 5 days. If adding a chili, mix it in when you eat the salad to prevent too much spiciness from developing while it marinates.

Ranch-Flavored Roasted Cashews

SERVES
3 TO 4

PREP TIME
5 MINUTES

COOK TIME
12 MINUTES

PER SERVING

CALORIES:
617

TOTAL FAT:
50 G

CARBS:
33 G

FIBER:
4 G

PROTEIN:
19 G

CALCIUM:
64 MG

VITAMIN D:
0 MCG

VITAMIN B12:
0 MCG

IRON:
7 MG

ZINC:
6 MG

I have always loved ranch-flavored anything, so when I went vegan, giving up ranch was a tough thing to do. One of the key ingredients in ranch seasoning is dried buttermilk powder, and for the longest time, I couldn't find a vegan workaround. One day, I simply tried omitting it and made ranch seasoning without it. To my surprise, it was just as delicious, so now I can enjoy it again!

1 tablespoon dried parsley
1 tablespoon dried dill
2 teaspoons onion powder
2 teaspoons garlic powder
1 teaspoon nutritional yeast

½ teaspoon salt
1 teaspoon ground black pepper
3 cups raw cashews
2 tablespoons extra-virgin olive oil

1. Preheat the oven to 350°F. Line a large baking sheet with parchment paper and set aside.

2. In a large bowl, make the ranch seasoning mix by combining the parsley, dill, onion powder, garlic powder, nutritional yeast, salt, and pepper.

3. Add the cashews and olive oil and toss to coat. Spread the seasoned cashews on the baking sheet in a single layer.

4. Bake for 12 minutes, stirring halfway through. Allow to cool before serving. Store in an airtight container.

VARIATION TIP: Turn the ranch seasoning mix from this recipe into a ranch dressing or dip. Combine the ranch seasoning mix with 1½ cups of Easy 4-Ingredient Vegan Mayonnaise (page 21), ¼ cup of unsweetened soy milk, 1½ teaspoons of vinegar or lemon juice, and 2 crushed garlic cloves.

Movie-Night Popcorn

SERVES
4

PREP TIME
5 MINUTES

My favorite thing about going to the movies has always been the popcorn. Our local movie theater now has shakers with flavored popcorn seasoning, but most of them aren't vegan. I created these vegan flavor seasonings so I could enjoy flavored popcorn, too. I originally came up with these seasonings to pair with cashew cheese, but I found they tasted amazing on popcorn. Whip up a batch and enjoy your movie night!

PER SERVING

CALORIES:
227

TOTAL FAT:
14 G

CARBS:
20 G

FIBER:
4 G

PROTEIN:
6 G

CALCIUM:
59 MG

VITAMIN D:
0 MCG

VITAMIN B12:
3 MCG

IRON:
3 MG

ZINC:
2 MG

For the nacho cheese seasoning mix

¼ cup nutritional yeast

1 teaspoon garlic powder

1 teaspoon onion powder

1 tablespoon paprika

1 teaspoon salt

¼ teaspoon turmeric

For the dill pickle seasoning mix

2½ tablespoons dried dill

2 tablespoons dried coriander

1 teaspoon dried mustard powder

1 teaspoon onion powder

1 teaspoon garlic powder

2 teaspoons salt

For the popcorn

¼ cup popcorn kernels

¼ cup melted vegan butter

3 tablespoons nacho cheese seasoning or dill pickle seasoning

TO MAKE THE NACHO CHEESE SEASONING MIX

In a small bowl, mix the nutritional yeast, garlic powder, onion powder, paprika, salt, and turmeric. Store in an airtight container.

TO MAKE THE DILL PICKLE SEASONING MIX

In a small bowl, mix the dried dill, dried coriander, dried mustard powder, onion powder, garlic powder, and salt. Store in an airtight container.

TO MAKE THE POPCORN

Pop the popcorn in an air popper and follow the manufacturer's directions. Toss with the melted butter and seasoning mix of your choice.

VARIATION TIP: Mix these seasonings into cashew cream cheese. To make cashew cream cheese, soak 3 cups of cashews for 1 hour. Drain and blend them in a food processor or high-speed blender with 1 teaspoon of salt, 1 tablespoon of lemon juice, and 3 tablespoons of seasoning.

BBQ Soy Jerky

Soy jerky is a great vegan alternative to traditional beef jerky and makes a great game-day snack or addition to a charcuterie or cheese board. Like traditional jerky, this version cooks low and slow to dry out the soy curls and give them that chewy texture. It takes more time than many of the recipes in this book, but it's a fairly low-maintenance dish—once it's in the oven, you're free to do other things while it cooks.

PER SERVING

CALORIES:
301

TOTAL FAT:
10 G

CARBS:
43 G

FIBER:
4 G

PROTEIN:
12 G

CALCIUM:
94 MG

VITAMIN D:
0 MCG

VITAMIN B12:
0 MCG

IRON:
2 MG

ZINC:
1 MG

½ cup Homemade BBQ Sauce (page 24)

4 cups boiling water

1 (8-ounce) package dried soy curls

1. Preheat the oven to 275°F. Line a large rimmed baking sheet with parchment paper.

2. Prepare the Homemade BBQ Sauce.

3. In a large bowl, whisk together the BBQ sauce and water. Add the soy curls and let them soak for 5 minutes, stirring occasionally, until most of the liquid is absorbed.

4. Drain off any excess liquid and spread the curls on the prepared baking sheet in a single layer. Bake for one hour, tossing every 15 minutes. Cool before serving and store in the refrigerator for up to 2 weeks.

STRETCH TIP: Because this jerky can be refrigerated for up to 2 weeks, it makes an excellent edible holiday gift. Divide a batch into 3 to 4 small (8-ounce) mason jars, tie them with decorative ribbons, and keep refrigerated until you need them.

Loaded Nachos

SERVES
4

PREP TIME
10 MINUTES

COOK TIME
15 MINUTES

Friday nights are nacho night at my house. At the end of a long week, there's nothing better than plopping down on the couch with the TV remote and a plate of warm, cheesy, chili-smothered goodness. This recipe is great for using up leftovers, so if you have them, go for the full nacho experience. If you don't have these toppings, make a pared-down version using whatever you have on hand, like beans or vegan Cheddar-style shreds.

2½ cups Hearty Vegetarian Chili (page 87)

2 cups Queso (page 32), divided

1 cup Pico de Gallo (page 23)

1 cup Roasted Garlic Guacamole (page 22)

1 (13-ounce) bag tortilla chips

3 scallions, finely chopped

¼ head iceberg lettuce, shredded

½ cup sliced black olives

½ cup vegan sour cream

PER SERVING

CALORIES:
698

TOTAL FAT:
36 G

CARBS:
85 G

FIBER:
17 G

PROTEIN:
16 G

CALCIUM:
241 MG

VITAMIN D:
0 MCG

VITAMIN B12:
2 MCG

IRON:
5 MG

ZINC:
3 MG

1. Preheat the oven to 375°F. Line a large baking sheet with aluminum foil or parchment paper.

2. Prepare the Hearty Vegetarian Chili, Queso, Pico de Gallo, and Roasted Garlic Guacamole (or assemble other leftovers).

3. Spread the tortilla chips out in a single layer on the baking sheet (though it's okay if some overlap a bit). Pour the vegetarian chili and one cup of queso over the chips. Bake for 15 minutes or until the queso is bubbly and the chips are golden.

4. Remove the baking sheet from the oven. Top the nachos with the pico de gallo, scallions, lettuce, and olives. Pour the remaining queso on top.

5. Serve with the sour cream and guacamole on the side.

VARIATION TIP: If you don't feel like making a full batch of chili for this dish, swap it out for 2 cups of Tofu Chorizo Crumble (page 16) instead. In a pinch, a can of baked or refried beans makes a good chili replacement here, too.

Trail Mix Cookies

SERVES
6

PREP TIME
10 MINUTES

COOK TIME
18 MINUTES

PER SERVING

CALORIES:
247

TOTAL FAT:
8 G

CARBS:
41 G

FIBER:
6 G

PROTEIN:
7 G

CALCIUM:
63 MG

VITAMIN D:
0 MCG

VITAMIN B12:
0 MCG

IRON:
2 MG

ZINC:
1 MG

These cookies are a great energy boost. They have no refined sugar, no added oils, and are flourless. If you swap the regular oats for certified gluten-free oats, they're also gluten-free. These are a healthy breakfast for adults and kids alike—but of course, then my kids go to school and tell their teachers they had cookies for breakfast, and I get the side-eye at after-school pick up. Maybe I should make the teachers a batch next time.

2 large ripe bananas
¼ cup unsweetened applesauce
2 tablespoons all-natural
   almond butter
½ teaspoon ground cinnamon
¼ teaspoon ground ginger
¼ teaspoon ground nutmeg
Zest of 1 medium orange

1 teaspoon vanilla extract
2 cups large-flake rolled oats
2 tablespoons ground flaxseed
   (optional)
1 tablespoon chia seeds (optional)
¼ cup raisins
¼ cup dried cranberries
⅓ cup sliced or slivered almonds

1. Preheat the oven to 350°F. Line a large baking sheet with parchment paper.

2. In a large bowl with a fork or mixing spoon, mash the bananas and applesauce together. Add the almond butter, cinnamon, ginger, nutmeg, orange zest, vanilla extract, rolled oats, ground flaxseed (if using), chia seeds (if using), raisins, cranberries, and almonds. Mix well until a chunky batter forms.

3. Using a ⅓-cup dry measure, scoop balls of dough onto the baking sheet. Flatten the balls to ½ inch thick. Bake the cookies until golden but not dark, about 18 minutes.

VARIATION TIP: If you don't have almond butter, swap it out for all-natural peanut butter or even tahini. Both will give the cookies a great nutty flavor and are just as sticky, which helps bind the batter together.

Eggplant Antipasto

SERVES
4 TO 6

PREP TIME
15 MINUTES

COOK TIME
25 MINUTES

This fairly simple antipasto knocks the socks off of anything store-bought. The briny olives and vinegar combined with the rich and bright tomato, eggplant, and peppers create an incredible spread that is delicious served on crostini as part of an upscale charcuterie board. The trick is to make sure that the vegetables are diced uniformly so that they finish cooking at the same time.

¼ cup extra-virgin olive oil

2 medium eggplants, peeled and cut into ½-inch cubes

1 medium onion, diced

1 medium green bell pepper, diced

3 celery stalks, diced

5 cloves garlic, minced

1 cup tomato purée, passata, or tomato sauce

¾ cup tomato paste

¾ cup pitted, sliced, kalamata olives

¾ cup chopped green olives

2 tablespoons red wine vinegar

¼ teaspoon oregano

Sriracha or other hot sauce, to taste

½ teaspoon salt

1 teaspoon ground black pepper

PER SERVING

CALORIES:
278

TOTAL FAT:
17 G

CARBS:
26 G

FIBER:
11 G

PROTEIN:
5 G

CALCIUM:
56 MG

VITAMIN D:
0 MCG

VITAMIN B12:
0 MCG

IRON:
2 MG

ZINC:
1 MG

1. Heat the olive oil in a large, deep skillet over medium heat. Add the eggplant, onion, bell pepper, and celery, and cook until the onions are translucent and the vegetables start to soften, about 5 minutes. Add the garlic and continue cooking for 2 minutes.

2. Add the tomato purée, tomato paste, kalamata olives, green olives, and red wine vinegar to the skillet, and mix to combine.

3. Bring the mixture to a quick boil, then immediately reduce heat to low and simmer, covered, for 30 minutes, stirring frequently.

4. Add the oregano, sriracha, salt, and pepper. Spread on crackers or crostini, or use as a sandwich spread. Refrigerate in an airtight container for up to a week.

VARIATION TIP: I've chosen eggplant, celery, and peppers for this one, but this recipe is easily adaptable to include other favorite veggies, like carrots, zucchini, pearl onions, mushrooms, and cauliflower.

Sweet Potato Hummus

SERVES
6 TO 8

PREP TIME
10 MINUTES
+ CHILL TIME

COOK TIME
20 MINUTES

PER SERVING

CALORIES:
186

TOTAL FAT:
9 G

CARBS:
22 G

FIBER:
6 G

PROTEIN:
6 G

CALCIUM:
74 MG

VITAMIN D:
0 MCG

VITAMIN B12:
0 MCG

IRON:
2 MG

ZINC:
1 MG

I love this twist on classic hummus. The sweet potatoes add a beautiful pop of color, and they provide a lovely, rich flavor as well. Sweet potato pairs well with the autumnal flavors in this dish, like cinnamon, nutmeg, and cumin. Try serving it on a vegetable platter at your next gathering. I like to dust the tops with a little extra smoked paprika or drizzle them with hot sauce and olive oil.

2 medium sweet potatoes
1 (15-ounce) can chickpeas, drained and rinsed
¼ cup tahini
3 garlic cloves
1 tablespoon nutritional yeast
1 tablespoon onion powder
½ teaspoon ground black pepper
½ teaspoon smoked paprika

¼ teaspoon ground cinnamon
¼ teaspoon nutmeg
¼ teaspoon ground cumin
½ teaspoon salt
1 tablespoon lemon juice
¼ to ½ teaspoon sriracha or other hot sauce
2 to 4 tablespoons extra-virgin olive oil

1. Using a fork or paring knife, poke holes over the entire surface of the sweet potatoes. Place on a microwave-safe plate and cook in the microwave on high for 12 to 15 minutes, or until the potatoes are tender. Slice open and set aside to cool slightly.

2. When cool enough to handle, scoop the sweet potato flesh out of the skins and transfer it to a food processor or blender.

3. Add the chickpeas, tahini, garlic, nutritional yeast, onion powder, pepper, paprika, cinnamon, nutmeg, cumin, salt, lemon juice, and sriracha to the food processor and process until smooth. While the food processor is running, slowly drizzle in the olive oil, 1 tablespoon at a time, until the mixture becomes a thick paste—slightly thicker than regular hummus. Serve or refrigerate for up to a week.

VARIATION TIP: Use this sweet potato hummus in place of plain hummus in a sandwich or wrap. It pairs beautifully with roasted vegetables or falafel or in *Soy Curl Shawarma Wraps* (page 60).

Veggie Fajita Layered Dip

SERVES
4 TO 6

PREP TIME
15 MINUTES

COOK TIME
10 MINUTES

I have had a love affair with fajitas for as long as I can remember. There's something so special about assembling each one individually, adding or leaving out whatever you like. This dip is an homage to fajitas and is great for using up basics featured elsewhere in this book. I sometimes give this recipe a twist by adding a layer of canned refried beans at the bottom.

PER SERVING

CALORIES:
750

TOTAL FAT:
46 G

CARBS:
77 G

FIBER:
16 G

PROTEIN:
18 G

CALCIUM:
415 MG

VITAMIN D:
1 MCG

VITAMIN B12:
2 MCG

IRON:
7 MG

ZINC:
4 MG

For the fajitas

2 cups Tofu Chorizo Crumble (page 16)

1 cup Stovetop Enchilada Sauce (page 26)

2 tablespoons extra-virgin olive oil

1 medium onion, diced

1 red bell pepper, diced

1 green bell pepper, diced

1 medium zucchini, diced

4 ounces cremini mushrooms, stemmed and caps thinly sliced

For the dip

2 cups Queso (page 32)

1 cup Pico de Gallo (page 23)

½ head iceberg lettuce, shredded

1 cup store-bought guacamole

2 cups vegan sour cream

½ cup sliced black olives, for garnish

4 scallions, finely chopped, for garnish

1 (13-ounce) bag tortilla chips

TO MAKE THE FAJITAS

1. Prepare the Tofu Chorizo Crumble and Stovetop Enchilada Sauce.

2. In a deep skillet, heat the oil over medium-high heat. Add the onion, bell peppers, zucchini, and mushrooms. Cook for 5 to 7 minutes, until the onions are translucent and the vegetables start to soften.

3. In a separate skillet, heat the Tofu Chorizo Crumble and enchilada sauce until warmed through, about 5 minutes. Add the chorizo and enchilada sauce to the vegetables.

CONTINUED >

TO MAKE THE DIP

1. Prepare the Queso and Pico de Gallo.

2. Place the veggie-chorizo mixture on the bottom of a large round serving bowl and top with the queso. Add a layer of shredded lettuce, then the guacamole, pico de gallo, and finally sour cream. Sprinkle the black olives and scallions on top. Serve with the tortilla chips.

VARIATION TIP: Don't feel like a chip-and-dip platter? Assemble the same components in large flour tortillas to make delicious layered burritos. If you have leftover rice in the fridge, add it in to make a healthy vegan version of Taco Bell's 7-Layer Burrito.

Spicy Hummus with Homemade Pita Crisps

SERVES
4 TO 6

PREP TIME
15 MINUTES

COOK TIME
10 MINUTES

This beautiful hummus platter is an elevated version of your usual veggies and dip. It combines the classic flavors of hummus (chickpeas, tahini, lemon, and salt) with a good dose of heat and is balanced by the cool, fresh crunch of a quick chopped salad. You can serve this with fresh pita or even store-bought pita chips, but it's actually quite simple to make your own, and it gives you extra bragging rights.

PER SERVING

CALORIES:
510

TOTAL FAT:
20 G

CARBS:
71 G

FIBER:
15 G

PROTEIN:
18 G

CALCIUM:
131 MG

VITAMIN D:
0 MCG

VITAMIN B12:
0 MCG

IRON:
5 MG

ZINC:
2 MG

For the pita chips

6 whole wheat pitas
2 tablespoons extra-virgin olive oil
½ teaspoon salt
½ teaspoon ground black pepper

For the hummus

2 (15-ounce) cans chickpeas, drained and rinsed, ¼ cup brine reserved
¼ cup tahini
⅓ cup, plus 2 tablespoons fresh lemon juice, divided

1 teaspoon salt, divided
1 teaspoon ground black pepper, divided
½ teaspoon sriracha
2 tablespoons extra-virgin olive oil
1 cup halved grape tomatoes, for topping
1 seedless cucumber, chopped small, for topping
¼ red onion, diced
2 to 3 tablespoons fresh flat-leaf parsley, minced

TO MAKE THE PITA CHIPS

Preheat the oven to 375°F. Line a large baking sheet with parchment paper. Cut each pita into quarters, then cut each quarter in half to yield 8 triangles. Spread the pita wedges on a baking sheet in an even layer. Drizzle with 2 tablespoons of olive oil and bake for 10 minutes or until crispy. Set aside to cool.

TO MAKE THE HUMMUS

1. In a food processor or blender, combine the chickpeas, tahini, ⅓ cup lemon juice, ½ teaspoon of salt, ½ teaspoon of ground black pepper, sriracha, and olive oil. Process until smooth. If the hummus is too thick, slowly stream in the reserved chickpea water until the desired creaminess is reached.

CONTINUED >

Spicy Hummus with Homemade Pita Crisps, CONTINUED

2. Make the chopped salad topping. In a large mixing bowl, combine the tomatoes, cucumber, onion, and parsley. Toss with the remaining 2 tablespoons of lemon juice, the remaining ½ teaspoon of salt, and the remaining ½ teaspoon of pepper.

3. Spread the hummus in a ½-inch layer at the center of a medium platter or large plate, leaving a ½-inch border. Place the chopped salad on top of the hummus and garnish the edges with the pita chips.

VARIATION TIP: Look online or at a specialty market for za'atar and sumac, two seasonings common in Middle Eastern cooking. Za'atar is a hearty spice mix that includes thyme, oregano, marjoram, and sesame seeds, among other spices; sprinkle it on the pita chips before baking. Sumac has a bright, lemony flavor and is fantastic mixed into the chopped salad in this recipe.

Nutty Chocolate Snack Mix

SERVES
6 TO 8

PREP TIME
15 MINUTES

This is a really fun "cheat" snack when you're looking for a once-in-a-while sweet treat. It's a vegan dessert take on classic Chex Mix—pretty much a kitchen sink of sweet and salty goodness. I typically bust this recipe out once or twice a year for special occasions that warrant sugary treats. This is essentially a no-bake recipe and requires only the microwave, so you can throw it together quickly when a craving strikes.

2 cups Rice Chex cereal

2 cups Corn Chex cereal

2 cups Chocolate Chex cereal

1 cup pecan halves

1 cup peanuts

½ cup crushed pretzels

1 cup dairy-free chocolate chips

1 cup vegan mini marshmallows, such as Dandies

½ cup packed brown sugar

¼ cup butter

5 tablespoons light corn syrup

¼ cup smooth peanut butter

½ teaspoon baking soda

½ cup powdered sugar, for dusting (optional)

PER SERVING

CALORIES:
705

TOTAL FAT:
42 G

CARBS:
77 G

FIBER:
5 G

PROTEIN:
13 G

CALCIUM:
126 MG

VITAMIN D:
34 MCG

VITAMIN B12:
1 MCG

IRON:
9 MG

ZINC:
4 MG

1. Line a large baking sheet with parchment paper. Set aside.

2. In a large mixing bowl, combine the rice, corn, and chocolate cereals, pecans, peanuts, pretzels, chocolate chips, and marshmallows.

3. In a large microwave-safe bowl, combine the brown sugar, butter, corn syrup, and peanut butter. Microwave on high for 2 minutes. Stir in the baking soda. Pour this mixture over the dry mixture and stir well to coat. Transfer to a baking sheet and dust with the powdered sugar, if using. Let cool before serving and store for up to a week in an airtight container.

VARIATION TIP: To give this recipe a holiday-themed twist, replace the peanuts, peanut butter, and marshmallows with roasted almonds, almond butter, and dried cranberries or cherries. Serve it at your winter holiday party or transfer to mason jars and give it as gifts.

Blueberry Hand Pies, 186

8

Desserts

Banana Bread

Is there anything better than the smell of banana bread baking in your oven? It makes the entire house smell heavenly. This classic recipe makes me feel better about having overripe bananas lying around. My kids won't touch bananas if they have even ONE freckle on them. If you make these as muffins instead, cut your baking time by half.

SERVES
6 TO 8

PREP TIME
10 MINUTES

COOK TIME
50 MINUTES

PER SERVING

CALORIES:
420

TOTAL FAT:
19 G

CARBS:
57 G

FIBER:
5 G

PROTEIN:
7 G

CALCIUM:
63 MG

VITAMIN D:
5 MCG

VITAMIN B12:
0 MCG

IRON:
2 MG

ZINC:
0 MG

1½ cups flour
1 teaspoon baking soda
1 teaspoon baking powder
¼ cup brown sugar
½ teaspoon salt
½ cup rolled oats
3 large ripe bananas
2 tablespoons ground flaxseed

⅓ cup unsweetened soy milk
⅓ cup vegetable oil
2 tablespoon maple syrup
1 tablespoon vanilla extract
1 cup mini dairy-free chocolate chips, divided (preferably Enjoy Life brand)

1. Preheat the oven to 350°F. Grease a loaf pan or line with parchment paper covering all 4 sides.

2. In a large bowl, combine the flour, baking soda, baking powder, brown sugar, salt, and rolled oats. Set aside.

3. In a medium bowl, mash the bananas until almost no chunks remain. Add the flaxseed, milk, oil, maple syrup, and vanilla extract. Stir to combine.

4. Slowly pour the wet ingredients into the dry ingredients and stir until just combined. Stir in ½ cup of the mini chocolate chips.

5. Pour the cake batter into the greased or lined pan and spread it out evenly. Sprinkle the remaining chocolate chips on top in an even layer. Bake for 50 minutes or until a toothpick inserted in the center of the cake comes out clean. Cool in the loaf pan for 10 minutes, then transfer to a wire rack to continue cooling.

VARIATION TIP: Add some texture and crunch to your banana bread by adding 1 cup of chopped pecans or walnuts to the batter before baking. Reserve a few extras to sprinkle on top.

Apple Crisp

SERVES
6

PREP TIME
10 MINUTES

COOK TIME
40 MINUTES

To me, an apple crisp is the perfect autumn dessert. I like to use a sturdy, slightly tart apple for this recipe, such as Honeycrisp. They are at their peak in mid-fall, at the height of apple season, and they lend a lovely sweet-but-tart flavor to this dish. Apple crisps usually don't contain other fruits, but I like to add dried cranberries for a surprise punch of tartness that complements the rich, crunchy topping.

½ cup vegan butter
6 large apples, diced large
1 cup dried cranberries
2 tablespoons granulated sugar
2 teaspoons ground
  cinnamon, divided
¼ teaspoon ground nutmeg

¼ teaspoon ground ginger
2 teaspoons lemon juice
1 cup all-purpose flour
1 cup rolled oats
1 cup brown sugar
¼ teaspoon salt

1. Preheat the oven to 350°F. Lightly grease an 8-inch square baking dish with butter or cooking spray.

2. Make the filling. In a large bowl, combine the apples, cranberries, granulated sugar, 1 teaspoon of cinnamon, the nutmeg, ginger, and lemon juice. Toss to coat. Transfer the apple mixture to the prepared baking dish.

3. Make the topping. In the same large bowl, now empty, combine the all-purpose flour, oats, brown sugar, and salt. Stir to combine. Add the butter and, using a pastry cutter (or two knives moving in a crisscross pattern), cut the butter into the flour and oat mixture until the butter is the size of small peas.

4. Spread the topping over the apples evenly, patting down slightly. Bake for 40 minutes or until golden and bubbly.

VARIATION TIP: For an extra crunchy topping, try adding chopped pecans.

PER SERVING

CALORIES:
488

TOTAL FAT:
9 G

CARBS:
101 G

FIBER:
10 G

PROTEIN:
5 G

CALCIUM:
50 MG

VITAMIN D:
0 MCG

VITAMIN B12:
0 MCG

IRON:
2 MG

ZINC:
1 MG

Secret Ingredient Chocolate Brownies

SERVES
6 TO 8

PREP TIME
10 MINUTES

COOK TIME
35 MINUTES

PER SERVING

CALORIES:
369

TOTAL FAT:
19 G

CARBS:
48 G

FIBER:
1 G

PROTEIN:
4 G

CALCIUM:
1 MG

VITAMIN D:
0 MCG

VITAMIN B12:
0 MCG

IRON:
1 MG

ZINC:
0 MG

My secret ingredient for these brownies is chickpea aquafaba. Loosely translated from Latin, *aquafaba* means "water-bean." Aquafaba is the viscous water that results from cooking beans. Yes, I'm referring to that canned bean water that so many of us pour down the drain. Aquafaba closely mimics the texture of egg whites, and unwhipped, it can be used in place of eggs in rich, dense desserts like these chewy brownies. One large egg is equivalent to 3 tablespoons of aquafaba.

¾ cup flour

¼ teaspoon baking soda

¼ teaspoon salt

⅓ cup vegan butter

¾ cup sugar

2 tablespoon water

1¼ cups semi-sweet or dark dairy-free chocolate chips

6 tablespoons aquafaba, divided

1 teaspoon vanilla extract

1. Preheat the oven to 325°F. Line a 9-inch square baking pan with parchment or grease well.

2. In a large bowl, combine the flour, baking soda, and salt. Set aside.

3. In a medium saucepan over medium-high heat, combine the butter, sugar, and water. Bring to a boil, stirring occasionally. Remove from heat and stir in the chocolate chips.

4. Whisk in 3 tablespoons of aquafaba until thoroughly combined. Add the vanilla extract and the remaining 3 tablespoons of aquafaba, and whisk until mixed.

5. Add the chocolate mixture into the flour mixture and stir until combined. Pour in an even layer into the prepared pan. Bake for 35 minutes, until the top is set but the brownie jiggles slightly when shaken. Allow to cool completely, 45 minutes to 1 hour, before removing and serving.

TECHNIQUE TIP: The brownies will look undercooked when they first come out of the oven. Resist the urge to bake them longer—they'll get too dry. Aquafaba sets differently than an egg, so as the brownies cool, they'll take on the rich chewiness of non-vegan brownies.

Chocolate Chip Pecan Cookies

MAKES
30 SMALL
COOKIES

PREP TIME
10 MINUTES

COOK TIME
16 MINUTES

PER COOKIE

CALORIES:
152

TOTAL FAT:
11 G

CARBS:
13 G

FIBER:
1 G

PROTEIN:
2 G

CALCIUM:
2 MG

VITAMIN D:
0 MCG

VITAMIN B12:
0 MCG

IRON:
0 MG

ZINC:
0 MG

These cookies are a delicious cross between shortbread and classic chocolate chip cookies. They are buttery and delicate like shortbread, but full of chocolate and pecan flavor. They're an upgraded vegan version of Keebler Pecan Sandies. To make these cookies nut-free, omit the pecans and use extra chocolate chips.

¾ cup pecan halves, toasted
1 cup vegan butter
½ teaspoon salt
½ cup powdered sugar

2 teaspoons vanilla extract
2 cups all-purpose flour
1 cup mini dairy-free chocolate chips, such as Enjoy Life brand

1. Preheat the oven to 350°F. Line a large rimmed baking sheet with parchment paper.

2. In a small skillet over medium heat, toast the pecans until warm and fragrant, about 2 minutes. Remove from the pan. Once these are cool, chop them into small pieces.

3. Using an electric hand mixer or a stand mixer fitted with a paddle attachment, combine the butter, salt, and powdered sugar, and cream together on high speed for 3 to 4 minutes, until light and fluffy. Add the vanilla extract and beat for 1 minute.

4. Turn the mixer on low and slowly add the flour, ½ cup at a time, until a dough forms. Add the chocolate chips and pecans, and mix until just incorporated.

5. Using your hands, a large spoon, or a 1-inch ice cream scoop, drop 1-inch balls of dough on the baking sheet, spaced 1 inch apart. Gently press down on the cookies to flatten them slightly.

6. Bake for 12 to 14 minutes until just golden around the edges. Cool on the baking sheet for 5 minutes before transferring them to a wire rack to cool. Serve or store in an airtight container.

PREP TIP: Roll any extra dough into a log, wrap it in plastic wrap, and place in a freezer-safe resealable bag or container. Defrost the dough in the fridge overnight before using.

Peanut Butter Chip Cookies

MAKES
12 TO 15
COOKIES

PREP TIME
10 MINUTES

COOK TIME
15 MINUTES

PER COOKIE

CALORIES:
192

TOTAL FAT:
12 G

CARBS:
17 G

FIBER:
3 G

PROTEIN:
6 G

CALCIUM:
22 MG

VITAMIN D:
0 MCG

VITAMIN B12:
0 MCG

IRON:
1 MG

ZINC:
0 MG

I love to make these cookies with my kids. It's a great weekend activity that helps get little hands used to working in a kitchen. These are sweetened with bananas and maple syrup, not refined sugar, so they're healthier for growing bodies, too. To completely omit processed ingredients of any kind, swap out the chocolate chips for raisins or dried cranberries.

1 tablespoon ground flaxseed
3 tablespoons hot water
1 cup rolled oats
1 teaspoon baking soda
1 teaspoon ground cinnamon
¼ teaspoon salt

1 ripe banana, mashed
¼ cup maple syrup
½ cup all-natural smooth
  peanut butter
1 tablespoon vanilla extract
½ cup dairy-free chocolate chips

1. Preheat the oven to 350°F. Line a large rimmed baking sheet with parchment paper.

2. Make a flaxseed egg by combining the ground flaxseed and hot water in a small bowl. Stir and let it sit for 5 minutes until thickened.

3. In a medium bowl, combine the oats, baking soda, cinnamon, and salt. Set aside.

4. In a large bowl, mash the banana and add the maple syrup, peanut butter, flaxseed egg, and vanilla extract. Stir to combine.

5. Add the dry mixture into the wet mixture and stir until just incorporated (do not overmix). Gently fold in the chocolate chips.

6. Using a large spoon or 2-inch ice cream scoop, drop the cookie dough balls onto the baking sheet. Flatten them slightly. Bake for 12 to 15 minutes or until the bottoms and edges are slightly browned. Serve or store in an airtight container.

SUBSTITUTION TIP: Try using tahini instead of peanut butter to give this treat a nut-free makeover. Tahini has a wonderfully nutty flavor when warmed and works just as well to hold these cookies together.

No-Bake Chocolate Coconut Energy Balls

MAKES
9 ENERGY
BALLS

PREP TIME
15 MINUTES,

+ CHILL TIME

This recipe provides a quick and healthy way to satisfy a chocolate craving. These no-bake chocolate coconut energy balls are flourless and free of refined sugar—they're sweetened with dates and maple syrup. They are also packed with high-protein ingredients like chia seeds, almond butter, pumpkin seeds, and sunflower seeds, making them the perfect chocolatey afternoon pick-me-up or morning snack.

¼ cup dry roasted or raw
   pumpkin seeds
¼ cup dry roasted or raw
   sunflower seeds
½ cup unsweetened
   shredded coconut
2 tablespoons chia seeds
¼ teaspoon salt

1½ tablespoons Dutch process
   cocoa powder
¼ cup rolled oats
2 tablespoons coconut oil, melted
6 pitted dates
2 tablespoons all-natural
   almond butter

1. In a food processor or blender, combine the pumpkin seeds, sun-flower seeds, coconut, chia seeds, salt, cocoa powder, and oats. Pulse until the mix is coarsely crumbled.

2. Add the coconut oil, dates, and almond butter. Pulse until the mixture is combined and sticks together when squeezed between your fingers.

3. Scoop out 2 tablespoons of mix at a time and roll them into 1½-inch balls with your hands. Place them spaced apart on a freezer-safe plate and freeze for 15 minutes. Remove from the freezer and keep refrigerated in an airtight container for up to 4 days.

VARIATION TIP: These energy balls are easy to customize using whatever you have in your pantry. Try using tahini or peanut butter and swapping out seeds for nuts like pecans, almonds, or cashews.

PER BALL

CALORIES:
230

TOTAL FAT:
12 G

CARBS:
27 G

FIBER:
5 G

PROTEIN:
5 G

CALCIUM:
48 MG

VITAMIN D:
0 MCG

VITAMIN B12:
0 MCG

IRON:
2 MG

ZINC:
1 MG

Blueberry Hand Pies

SERVES
6 TO 8

PREP TIME
20 MINUTES,
+ CHILL TIME

COOK TIME
20 MINUTES

What's better than a fresh, homemade blueberry pie? Not having to share it, of course! These hand pies are the perfect portable dessert and are nowhere near as messy as a traditional pie slice. They are very convenient for taking to summer get-togethers. I'm partial to blueberry, but you can use whatever fruit is in season. Strawberries, peaches, apples, and blackberries all make great fillings for this recipe.

PER SERVING

CALORIES:
416

TOTAL FAT:
23 G

CARBS:
46 G

FIBER:
5 G

PROTEIN:
6 G

CALCIUM:
12 MG

VITAMIN D:
4 MCG

VITAMIN B12:
0 MCG

IRON:
2 MG

ZINC:
0 MG

3 cups all-purpose flour, plus extra for dusting work surface
½ teaspoon salt
¼ cup, plus 2 tablespoons granulated sugar, divided
1 cup vegan butter
½ cup cold water

1 cup fresh blueberries
2 teaspoons lemon zest
2 teaspoons lemon juice
¼ teaspoon ground cinnamon
1 teaspoon cornstarch
¼ cup unsweetened soy milk
Coarse sugar, for sprinkling

1. Preheat the oven to 375°F. Line a large baking sheet with parchment paper. Set aside.

2. In a large bowl, combine the flour, salt, 2 tablespoons of granulated sugar, and vegan butter. Using a pastry cutter or two knives moving in a crisscross pattern, cut the butter into the other ingredients until the butter is the size of small peas.

3. Add the cold water and knead to form a dough. Tear the dough in half and wrap the halves separately in plastic wrap. Refrigerate for 15 minutes.

4. Make the blueberry filling. In a medium bowl, combine the blueberries, lemon zest, lemon juice, cinnamon, cornstarch, and the remaining ¼ cup of sugar.

5. Remove one half of the dough. On a floured surface, roll out the dough to ¼- to ½-inch thickness. Turn a 5-inch bowl upside down, and, using it as a guide, cut the dough into circles to make mini pie crusts. Reroll scrap dough to cut out more circles. Repeat with the second half of the dough. You should end up with 10 to 12 circles. Place the circles on the prepared sheet pan.

6. Spoon 1½ tablespoons of blueberry filling onto each circle, leaving a ¼-inch border. Fold the circles in half to cover the filling, forming a half-moon shape. Use a fork to press the edges of the dough to seal the pies.

7. When all the pies are assembled, use a paring knife to score the pies by cutting three lines through the top crusts. Brush each pie with soy milk and sprinkle with coarse sugar. Bake for 20 minutes or until the filling is bubbly and the tops are golden. Let cool before serving.

VARIATION TIP: Turn these hand pies into a savory dish and serve as an appetizer. Make the dough as the recipe instructs, omitting the sugar, and fill with your favorite savory filling, such as Tofu Chorizo Crumble (page 16), vegan Pepper Jack-style shreds, or sautéed spinach and mushrooms.

Date Squares

SERVES
12

PREP TIME
20 MINUTES

COOK TIME
25 MINUTES

PER SERVING

CALORIES:
443

TOTAL FAT:
12 G

CARBS:
81 G

FIBER:
7 G

PROTEIN:
5 G

CALCIUM:
51 MG

VITAMIN D:
0 MCG

VITAMIN B12:
0 MCG

IRON:
2 MG

ZINC:
0 MG

I grew up in Canada, and date squares are a quintessential Canadian dessert. Good food knows no borders, though, and these squares are delicious no matter what part of the world you live in. The crumbly base and topping perfectly complement the sticky, sweet dates inside. Typically served with coffee, date squares are a great dessert to serve at brunch or as a treat to accompany an afternoon coffee break.

Cooking spray, for greasing
1½ cups rolled oats
1½ cups all-purpose flour
¾ cup, plus ⅓ cup brown
    sugar, divided
½ teaspoon ground cinnamon
¼ teaspoon ground nutmeg

1 teaspoon baking soda
¼ teaspoon salt
¾ cup vegan butter
18 pitted dates
1 teaspoon lemon zest
1 teaspoon lemon juice
1 cup water

1. Preheat the oven to 350°F. Lightly grease or spray a 9-inch square baking dish. Set aside.

2. Make the base and topping mixture. In a large bowl, combine the rolled oats, flour, ¾ cup of brown sugar, cinnamon, nutmeg, baking soda, and salt. Add the butter and, using a pastry cutter or two knives working in a crisscross motion, cut the butter into the mixture to form a crumbly dough. Press half of the dough into the prepared baking dish and set the remaining half aside.

3. To make the date filling, place a small saucepan over medium heat. Add the dates, the remaining ⅓ cup of sugar, the lemon zest, lemon juice, and water. Bring to a boil and cook for 7 to 10 minutes, until thickened.

4. When cooked, pour the date mixture over the dough base in the baking dish and top with the remaining crumb dough. Gently press down and spread evenly to cover all the filling. Bake for 25 minutes until lightly golden on top. Cool before serving. Store in an airtight container.

VARIATION TIP: This recipe is also delicious with other fruit fillings, like mixed berries, strawberries and rhubarb, peaches, or apples. Simply swap the dates for your fruit of choice, adding 1 to 2 teaspoons of cornstarch if necessary to thicken the filling as it cooks.

Crazy Chocolate Cake

SERVES
12

PREP TIME
10 MINUTES

COOK TIME
35 MINUTES

Crazy cake, Wacky Cake, Depression Cake—versions of this recipe have been around for decades—as far back as the Great Depression, when ingredients like butter, milk, and eggs were scarce. Over time, this cake has transformed from a budget-friendly recipe to a dietary and allergen-friendly staple, since all the ingredients are "accidentally" vegan. I've included a vegan frosting recipe here as well.

For the cake

Cooking spray, for greasing

1½ cups all-purpose flour

1 cup granulated sugar

¼ cup Dutch process cocoa powder

1 teaspoon baking soda

½ teaspoon salt

1 teaspoon white vinegar

5 tablespoons vegetable oil

1 teaspoon vanilla extract

1 cup water

For the frosting

6 cups powdered sugar

1 cup cocoa powder

2 cups vegan butter, softened

1 teaspoon vanilla extract

1 pinch salt

PER SERVING

CALORIES:
831

TOTAL FAT:
44 G

CARBS:
111 G

FIBER:
6 G

PROTEIN:
5 G

CALCIUM:
15 MG

VITAMIN D:
0 MCG

VITAMIN B12:
0 MCG

IRON:
2 MG

ZINC:
1 MG

TO MAKE THE CAKE

1. Preheat the oven to 350°F. Grease or spray an 8-inch square baking dish or a 9-inch round cake pan.

2. In a large bowl, combine the flour, sugar, cocoa powder, baking soda, and salt. Add the vinegar, vegetable oil, vanilla extract, and water directly to the dry ingredients. Stir the batter until no lumps remain.

3. Pour the batter into the greased dish and bake for 35 minutes or until a toothpick inserted into the center comes out clean.

4. Once the cake is baked, cool it in the pan for 10 minutes. Transfer it to a plate and refrigerate for about 30 minutes, then frost (see instructions).

TO MAKE THE FROSTING

1. While the cake is baking, combine the powdered sugar and cocoa powder in a large bowl. Use an electric hand mixer or a stand mixer with the paddle attachment to beat the vegan butter on medium-high speed until pale and creamy.

CONTINUED >

Crazy Chocolate Cake, **CONTINUED**

2. Reduce the mixer speed to medium and add the powdered sugar and cocoa mix, ½ cup at a time, mixing well between each addition (about 5 minutes total).

3. Add the vanilla extract and salt and mix on high speed for 1 minute.

TECHNIQUE TIP: Double the cake and frosting recipes for a two-layer birthday cake. Divide the cake batter into two 9-inch pans and bake side by side in the oven. Cool completely. Add a layer of frosting on top of one cake, stack the other on top, and frost the entire cake. Add some sprinkles for an extra-special treat.

Chunky Chocolate Peanut Butter Balls

SERVES
6

PREP TIME
15 MINUTES
+ CHILL TIME

Energy bites are everywhere nowadays, and for good reason. They pack a ton of protein into a tiny morsel to make the perfect sweet-but-nutritious snack. After all, sometimes you want "just a little bite" of dessert. My kids love these in their lunches—they think they're getting a sweet treat, and I know they're getting energy to fuel their day. To make these nut-free, swap the peanut butter for seed butter or tahini.

½ cup crunchy peanut butter

1½ cups shredded coconut, divided

1 cup rolled oats

½ cup ground flaxseed

¼ cup chia seeds

½ cup dairy-free mini chocolate chips

⅓ cup maple syrup

1 teaspoon vanilla extract

1. Melt the peanut butter in a microwave-safe dish for 15 to 20 seconds.

2. In a large bowl, combine 1 cup of the shredded coconut, the rolled oats, ground flaxseed, chia seeds, and chocolate chips. Pour in the melted peanut butter, maple syrup, and vanilla extract. Stir well to combine. Refrigerate for 15 to 20 minutes, until chilled enough that the mixture sticks together when pressed but not so cold that the peanut butter hardens.

3. Place the remaining ½ cup of shredded coconut into a shallow dish. Spoon out 2 tablespoons of the mixture at a time and roll into 1-inch balls. Roll the balls in the remaining ½ cup of shredded coconut to coat. Refrigerate for up to a week.

VARIATION TIP: Try swapping out the peanut butter for almond butter and chopped almonds for a different but equally delicious flavor profile. You could also grate some lemon or orange zest in to brighten it up. Both citrus fruits pair really well with almond.

PER BALL

CALORIES:
528

TOTAL FAT:
35 G

CARBS:
47 G

FIBER:
12 G

PROTEIN:
12 G

CALCIUM:
99 MG

VITAMIN D:
0 MCG

VITAMIN B12:
0 MCG

IRON:
3 MG

ZINC:
1 MG

No-Churn Ice Cream

SERVES
2 TO 3

PREP TIME
5 MINUTES

COOK TIME
35 MINUTES

I scream, you scream, we all scream . . . well, you know the rest. I'm obsessed with this recipe for fresh, rich, fruity ice cream you can make without an ice cream machine and with just three ingredients. It does take some time to make homemade condensed coconut milk (the key ingredient in this recipe), but it can be made ahead. If you don't want to make condensed coconut milk, you can usually find it online.

CONDENSED COCONUT MILK PER SERVING

CALORIES:
843

TOTAL FAT:
59 G

CARBS:
63 G

FIBER:
0 G

PROTEIN:
5 G

CALCIUM:
80 MG

IRON:
4 MG

ZINC:
1 MG

RASPBERRY ICE CREAM PER SERVING

CALORIES:
328

TOTAL FAT:
20 G

CARBS:
32 G

FIBER:
4 G

PROTEIN:
3 G

CALCIUM:
47 MG

IRON:
2 MG

ZINC:
1 MG

For the homemade condensed coconut milk

(yields one cup of condensed milk)
1 (14-ounce) can coconut milk
¼ cup maple syrup

For the raspberry no-churn ice cream

1 cup (8 ounces) frozen raspberries
1 cup homemade condensed coconut milk

For the tropical fruit no-churn ice cream

1 cup (8 ounces) mixed frozen mango, pineapple, and peaches
1 cup homemade condensed coconut milk

For the chocolate cherry no-churn ice cream

1 cup (8 ounces) frozen cherries
1 cup homemade condensed coconut milk
2 to 3 tablespoons vegan chocolate syrup (or ½ cup dairy-free chocolate chips)

TO MAKE THE HOMEMADE CONDENSED COCONUT MILK

In a small saucepan, bring the coconut milk just to a boil, whisking constantly and watching carefully to make sure it doesn't boil over. Immediately reduce heat to a simmer and whisk in the maple syrup until dissolved. Cook for 30 to 35 minutes, whisking occasionally, until the mix reduces by half and darkens slightly. Cool completely.

TO MAKE THE RASPBERRY NO-CHURN ICE CREAM

Combine the frozen raspberries and condensed coconut milk in a food processor or high-speed blender and process until creamy. Serve immediately as soft-serve ice cream or transfer to an airtight, freezer-safe container and chill for 3 to 4 hours, until firm.

TO MAKE THE TROPICAL FRUIT NO-CHURN ICE CREAM

Combine the frozen mango, pineapple, peaches, and condensed coconut milk in a food processor or high-speed blender and process until creamy. Serve immediately as soft-serve ice cream or transfer to an airtight, freezer-safe container and chill for 3 to 4 hours, until firm.

TO MAKE THE CHOCOLATE CHERRY NO-CHURN ICE CREAM

Combine the frozen cherries and condensed coconut milk in a food processor or high-speed blender and process until creamy. When almost done, pour in the chocolate syrup (or chocolate chips) and process until fully incorporated. Serve immediately as soft-serve ice cream or transfer to an air-tight, freezer-safe container and chill for 3 to 4 hours, until firm.

STRETCH TIP: Condensed coconut milk will keep in the refrigerator for up to a week, so it's a great make-ahead item. It also works well in other recipes or drinks that call for condensed milk or heavy cream.

TROPICAL FRUIT ICE CREAM PER SERVING

CALORIES:
319

TOTAL FAT:
20 G

CARBS:
30 G

FIBER:
2 G

PROTEIN:
2 G

CALCIUM:
38 MG

IRON:
2 MG

ZINC:
0 MG

CHOCOLATE CHERRY ICE CREAM PER SERVING

CALORIES:
507

TOTAL FAT:
32 G

CARBS:
50 G

FIBER:
1 G

PROTEIN:
5 G

CALCIUM:
33 MG

IRON: 1 MG

ZINC: 0 MG

Chocolate Peanut Butter Crispy Bars

SERVES
6 TO 8

PREP TIME
20 MINUTES
+ CHILL TIME

PER SERVING

CALORIES:
977

TOTAL FAT:
66 G

CARBS:
83 G

FIBER:
11 G

PROTEIN:
26 G

CALCIUM:
70 MG

VITAMIN D:
0 MCG

VITAMIN B12:
0 MCG

IRON:
3 MG

ZINC:
1 MG

This no-bake treat is sure to be a crowd-pleaser at your next get-together. It's great for parties, BBQs, or even holiday cookie exchanges. The base is a no-bake brownie made from cashews and dates, which add fiber and protein and eliminate the need for refined sugar. Choosing all-natural peanut butters for this recipe also helps keep this lower in sugar and higher in protein.

1 cup dates

1 cup raw cashews

¼ cup Dutch process cocoa powder

1 teaspoon vanilla extract

1½ cups crunchy peanut butter

2 cups dairy-free chocolate chips

1 cup all-natural smooth peanut butter

3 cups puffed rice cereal, such as Rice Krispies

1. Line an 8-inch square baking dish with parchment paper. Set aside.

2. Soak the dates in a bowl of warm water for 10 minutes. Drain and pat dry.

3. In a food processor or blender, combine the dates, cashews, cocoa powder, and vanilla extract and process to form a thick dough. Press into the baking dish. Cover with the crunchy peanut butter, spreading it into an even layer. Refrigerate for 5 minutes.

4. In a large microwave-safe bowl, combine the chocolate chips and smooth peanut butter. Microwave in 30-second increments, stirring in between, until smooth. Remove from the microwave and stir in the puffed rice cereal, mixing to coat.

5. Pour the puffed rice mixture over the chunky peanut butter layer in the baking dish and press flat. Refrigerate for at least 30 minutes. Remove from the pan and cut into squares.

VARIATION TIP: To give this dessert a lighter, cakier feel, try swapping out the date and cashew base for brownies. Simply prepare your favorite brownie mix according to package directions (use flaxseed and water instead of an egg to make it vegan), allow to cool, and use in this recipe.

Frozen Chocolate Banana Bites 3 Ways

SERVES
4

PREP TIME
15 MINUTES
+ CHILL TIME

I love making these as an after-school snack for my kids. They're easy for little hands to grasp and feel like a special treat. At the same time, they're high in fiber and protein and low in refined sugar. Most of these ingredients are likely already in your pantry. The trick with this recipe is to freeze the bananas before using—it makes them easier to work with and less likely to slip.

For the chocolate peanut butter banana bites

⅓ cup all-natural smooth peanut butter

4 bananas, sliced into ½-inch rounds

½ cup chocolate chips

1 teaspoon coconut oil

For the chocolate strawberry bites

⅓ cup strawberry jam

4 bananas, sliced into ½-inch rounds

½ cup chocolate chips

1 teaspoon coconut oil

For the chocolate coconut bites

⅓ cup all-natural almond butter

4 bananas, sliced into ½-inch rounds

½ cup chocolate chips

1 teaspoon coconut oil

½ cup shredded coconut

CHOCOLATE PEANUT BUTTER BANANA BITES PER SERVING

CALORIES:
388

TOTAL FAT:
21 G

CARBS:
48 G

FIBER:
4 G

PROTEIN:
8 G

CALCIUM:
19 MG

VITAMIN D:
0 MCG

VITAMIN B12:
0 MCG

IRON:
1 MG

ZINC:
0 MG

TO MAKE THE CHOCOLATE PEANUT BUTTER BANANA BITES

1. Line a standard-size baking sheet with parchment paper. Spread a layer of peanut butter on half of the banana slices. Top with the remaining banana slices to form banana "sandwiches." Place on the prepared baking sheet and freeze for 1 hour.

2. While the bananas are freezing, combine the chocolate chips and coconut oil in a microwave-safe bowl. Microwave in 30-second increments, stirring in between, until smooth.

3. Dip each frozen banana sandwich halfway into the chocolate sauce and place them back on the baking sheet. Freeze again for 15 to 30 more minutes or until the chocolate is hardened. Serve and keep the leftovers frozen.

CONTINUED >

CHOCOLATE
STRAWBERRY
BITES PER
SERVING

CALORIES:
329

TOTAL FAT:
10 G

CARBS:
60 G

FIBER:
3 G

PROTEIN:
3 G

CALCIUM:
6 MG

VITAMIN D:
0 MCG

VITAMIN B12:
0 MCG

IRON:
0 MG

ZINC:
0 MG

Frozen Chocolate Banana Bites 3 Ways, CONTINUED

TO MAKE THE CHOCOLATE STRAWBERRY BITES

1. Line a standard-size baking sheet with parchment paper. Spoon a small amount of strawberry jam on half of the banana slices. Top with the remaining banana slices to form banana "sandwiches." Place on the prepared baking sheet and freeze for one hour.

2. Combine the chocolate chips and coconut oil in a microwave-safe bowl. Microwave in 30-second increments until smooth.

3. Dip each banana sandwich halfway into the chocolate sauce and place them back on the baking sheet. Freeze for 15 to 30 minutes or until the chocolate is hardened. Serve and keep the leftovers frozen.

TO MAKE THE CHOCOLATE COCONUT BITES

1. Line a standard-size baking sheet with parchment paper. Spread a layer of almond butter on half of the banana slices. Top with the remaining banana slices to form banana "sandwiches." Place on the prepared baking sheet and freeze for one hour.

2. Combine the chocolate chips and coconut oil in a microwave-safe bowl. Microwave in 30-second increments until smooth.

3. Dip each banana sandwich halfway into the chocolate sauce, sprinkle with shredded coconut, and place them back on the baking sheet. Freeze for 15 to 30 minutes or until the chocolate is hardened. Serve and keep leftovers frozen.

VARIATION TIP: You can use all kinds of toppings to coat the chocolate-covered side of the bananas after dipping them. I used shredded coconut in this recipe, but you can also use crushed peanuts or almonds or even rainbow sprinkles.

CHOCOLATE
COCONUT BITES
PER SERVING

CALORIES:
580

TOTAL FAT:
40 G

CARBS:
54 G

FIBER:
9 G

PROTEIN:
10 G

CALCIUM:
78 MG

VITAMIN D:
0 MCG

VITAMIN B12:
0 MCG

IRON:
1 MG

ZINC:
1 MG

Cranberry Orange Pound Cake

This show-stopping loaf pound cake will spruce up any holiday brunch. It's great year-round, but the flavor combination of cranberry and orange feels wintery to me, so I tend to save it for the holidays. This rich cake uses oranges twice: first soaked in an orange simple syrup, then topped with an orange glaze. I like to decorate the loaf with sugar-dusted cranberries and orange slices so my guests instantly know what flavor the cake is.

2 cups fresh cranberries

2 tablespoons, plus 1⅓ cups sugar, divided

1 cup plain coconut yogurt

1 large banana, mashed

2 teaspoons grated orange zest

1 teaspoon vanilla extract

½ cup vegetable oil

1½ cups all-purpose flour

2 teaspoons baking powder

½ teaspoon salt

⅓ cup, plus 2 tablespoons freshly squeezed orange juice

1 cup powdered sugar

1. Preheat the oven to 350°F. Grease a standard-size loaf pan. Line the bottom with parchment paper lengthwise, letting some hang over the edges. Set aside.

2. Mix the cranberries and 2 tablespoons of granulated sugar in a food processor or blender until coarsely chopped. Set aside.

3. In a large bowl, whisk together the yogurt, 1 cup of sugar, the banana, orange zest, vanilla extract, and oil. Stir in the cranberry mixture.

4. In a medium bowl, combine the flour, baking powder, and salt. Slowly incorporate the dry mixture into the wet mixture until smooth.

5. Pour the batter into the loaf pan and bake for 50 minutes, or until a toothpick inserted in the center comes out clean.

6. While the cake bakes, make the orange simple syrup. Combine the remaining ⅓ cup of sugar and ⅓ cup of orange juice in a small saucepan over medium heat. Simmer until the sugar dissolves and the syrup is clear. Set aside.

SERVES
6 TO 8

PREP TIME
15 MINUTES

COOK TIME
50 MINUTES

PER SERVING

CALORIES:
536

TOTAL FAT:
15 G

CARBS:
99 G

FIBER:
6 G

PROTEIN:
3 G

CALCIUM:
133 MG

VITAMIN D:
23 MCG

VITAMIN B12:
0 MCG

IRON:
1 MG

ZINC:
0 MG

CONTINUED >

7. Remove the cake from oven and let cool for 10 minutes. Remove from the loaf pan and place on a wire rack on top of a rimmed baking sheet to catch the syrup. Pour the simple syrup over the cake. Let cool completely.

8. Make the orange glaze. In a medium bowl, whisk the powdered sugar and the remaining 2 tablespoons of orange juice until no lumps remain. Drizzle over the cooled cake. Serve and store leftovers in an airtight container.

STRETCH TIP: Without the fruit, this is a great basic pound cake recipe that you can use for any occasion. Use this cake in trifles or parfaits, or use day-old slices to make the ultimate French toast.

Strawberry Rhubarb Coffee Cake

SERVES
6 TO 8

PREP TIME
20 MINUTES

COOK TIME
45 MINUTES

Don't let this recipe's long ingredient list and multiple steps intimidate you. This is a fantastic cake that highlights the sweet-yet-tart combination of strawberry and rhubarb. It's also a great recipe for summer, when both are in season. My best friend used to have a wild rhubarb patch in her garden, and she always brought me bags of fresh rhubarb. I'd make this cake for her in return. It was definitely a win-win situation.

For the filling

2 cups rhubarb, thinly sliced
2 cups strawberries, sliced
1 tablespoon lemon juice
⅔ cup granulated sugar
3 tablespoons cornstarch

For the cake

1½ cups all-purpose flour
¼ teaspoon baking soda
1 teaspoon baking powder
¼ teaspoon salt

¼ cup vegan butter, softened
¾ cup granulated sugar
½ cup coconut yogurt
1 banana, mashed
1 teaspoon vanilla extract

For the topping

¾ cup all-purpose flour
½ cup granulated sugar
½ teaspoon ground cinnamon
¼ teaspoon ground nutmeg
5 tablespoons melted butter

PER SERVING

CALORIES:
479

TOTAL FAT:
14 G

CARBS:
86 G

FIBER:
5 G

PROTEIN:
5 G

CALCIUM:
94 MG

VITAMIN D:
0 MCG

VITAMIN B12:
0 MCG

IRON:
2 MG

ZINC:
0 MG

TO MAKE THE FILLING

1. Set a medium saucepan over medium heat. Add the rhubarb, strawberries, lemon juice, sugar, and cornstarch and stir to combine.

2. Bring to a simmer, then reduce the heat to low and continue simmering until thickened, stirring often, for 5 to 7 minutes. Remove the filling from heat and let cool.

TO MAKE THE CAKE

1. Combine the flour, baking soda, baking powder, and salt in a small bowl. Set aside.

CONTINUED >

Strawberry Rhubarb Coffee Cake, CONTINUED

2. Using an electric hand mixer and a large bowl or a stand mixer with the paddle attachment, combine the butter and sugar and beat on high until light and fluffy, about 5 minutes. Add the yogurt, banana, and vanilla extract and beat until combined. Reduce the speed to low and slowly add the dry mixture until fully incorporated.

3. Pour the batter evenly into a prepared pan. Top with cooled strawberry-rhubarb filling and set aside.

TO MAKE THE TOPPING

In a medium bowl, combine the flour, sugar, cinnamon, nutmeg, and butter. Stir to form a crumble topping. Sprinkle evenly over the filling.

TO BAKE

Bake for 45 minutes or until a toothpick inserted in the center comes out clean and the topping is browned. Let cool for 10 minutes and serve or store in an airtight container.

VARIATION TIP: Make this cake year-round by swapping out the strawberries and rhubarb for whatever fruit is in season. Try using blueberries, blackberries, apples and cinnamon, or even cherries.

MEASUREMENT CONVERSIONS

VOLUME EQUIVALENTS (LIQUID)

US Standard (ounces)	US Standard (approximate)	Metric
2 tablespoons	1 fl.oz.	30 mL
¼ cup	2 fl. oz.	60 mL
½ cup	4 fl. oz.	120 mL
1 cup	8 fl. oz.	240 mL
1½ cups	12 fl.oz.	355 mL
2 cups or 1 pint	16 fl. oz.	475 mL
4 cups or 1 quart	32 fl. oz.	1 L
1 gallon	128 fl.oz.	4 L

OVEN TEMPERATURES

Fahrenheit (F)	Celsius (C) (approximate)
250°F	120°C
300°F	150°C
325°F	165°C
350°F	180°C
375°F	190°C
400°F	200°C
425°F	220°C
450°F	230°C

WEIGHT EQUIVALENTS

US Standard	Metric (approximate)
⅛ teaspoon	0.5 mL
¼ teaspoon	1 mL
½ teaspoon	2 mL
¾ teaspoon	4 mL
1 teaspoon	5 mL
1 tablespoon	15 mL
¼ cup	59 mL
⅓ cup	79 mL
½ cup	118 mL
⅔ cup	156 mL
¾ cup	177 mL
1 cup	235 mL
2 cups or 1 pint	475 mL
3 cups	700 mL
4 cups or 1 quart	1 L

VOLUME EQUIVALENTS (DRY)

US Standard	Metric (approximate)
½ ounce	15 g
1 ounce	30 g
2 ounces	60 g
4 ounces	115 g
8 ounces	225 g
12 ounces	340 g
16 ounces or 1 pound	455 g

Roasted Veg Ratatouille on Creamy Polenta, 114

INDEX

ACKNOWLEDGMENTS

Creating this book involved the work of a large team of people dedicated to making this project a success. Writing and publishing a book is a collaborative effort, and I'm grateful for the opportunity to work with such an amazing team to bring this book to life.

My most heartfelt thanks to the team at Callisto Media for their work on and belief in this book. To Vanessa Putt for giving me the opportunity to write this book and especially to Claire Yee, my managing editor, who was by my side through the entire process and made writing this book so easy. Thanks for all your inspiring words, line edits, and enthusiasm.

To my developmental editor, Allie Kiekhofer, thank you for ensuring this book "works" and for making my recipes come alive. To Holly, Ashley, Jill, Karen, and marketing—thank you for all your hard work to build and promote this book. Your efforts are truly appreciated.

ABOUT THE AUTHOR

Ally Lazare is a Toronto-based food blogger, writer, and home cook. She published her first book, *Ally's Kitchen: Comfort Food—100 Easy, Plant-Based Recipes for Everyone* in 2019.

Ally has been cooking and baking since she was in her teens, and after turning to a plant-based lifestyle in 2011, she began creating plant-based versions of all her favorite dishes.

When she's not cooking, Ally is busy collecting vintage cookbooks and retro kitchenware and spending time with her husband and two young daughters. You can follow Ally's culinary journeys on Instagram at @allylazare.